Englisch – Mittelstufe
Wir üben Grammatik

von H. Gumtau / W. Kurschatke / G. Kirsch

Lösungen zu den Tests (Manzbuch 297)

Manz Verlag München

Wir üben den Gebrauch der Zeiten

9.

will be; to get; have been; know; lives; invited; to spend; has; has placed; passed; got; have already done; have not yet seen; congratulated; Do you remember; found; should write; am looking forward.

10.

a) My uncle has lived in London for ten years.
b) Every day I help my aunt with the housework.
c) Last week I also went shopping for her.
d) I was just reading the Times when my uncle came home.
e) After I had spent a week in London I went to Dover for two days.
f) When I reached the station, my train was just leaving.
g) I have been learning English since 1976.

11.

a) will go; will invite
b) am going to see; will come; will bring
c) has just left; left
d) has been; was
e) got; had passed; got
f) is having; understands; remembers; learnt; will be

ENGLISCH MITTELSTUFE

WIR ÜBEN

GRAMMATIK

Übungen und Tests für das 8. bis 10. Schuljahr

von Hannes Gumtau, Wolfgang Kurschatke und Günter Kirsch

MANZ VERLAG MÜNCHEN

Herausgegeben von Ute Kretschmann

Manzbuch 297

11 10 9 1987 86 85 84
Die jeweils letzte Zahl bezeichnet die Auflage bzw. das Erscheinungsjahr

 · Umschlagentwurf: Ingeburg Rothemund, München · Gesamtherstellung: Verlag und Druckerei G. J. Manz AG, München/Dillingen · Printed in Germany

ISBN 3-7863-0297-9

Inhalt

A) Prüfungsvorbereitung

Liebe Schülerinnen und Schüler!

ENGLISCH MITTELSTUFE – Wir üben GRAMMATIK enthält Texte, Übungen, Lernhilfen und Comprehension Tests für die 8. bis 10. Jahrgangsstufen. Es ist also eine Hilfe für alle, die sich auf den Mittleren Schulabschluß vorbereiten:

- Es werden nicht nur die Stoffinhalte der 8. bis 10. Klassen geübt, sondern auch solche aus früheren Jahren aufgefrischt, weil sie bei Prüfungen unerläßlich sind.
- Die Übungen entsprechen den typischen Fragestellungen bei schriftlichen Arbeiten.
- Sie können sowohl im Klassenverband als auch im Selbststudium durchgearbeitet werden. Die Lernhilfen und Lösungsvorschläge ermöglichen eine konsequente Überprüfung der eigenen Leistungen.

Das Übungsbuch ist so angelegt, daß ihr in relativ knapper Zeit die wichtigen Themenkreise intensiv üben und sichern könnt. Die allgemeinen und die speziellen Lernhilfen gehen stets auf Fragen ein, die im Unterricht häufig auftauchen. Sie können natürlich nur als Hinweis und Anregung dienen.
Zur völligen Aufklärung eines Sachverhalts solltet ihr bei Bedarf in eurem Lehrwerk, eventuell im Wörterbuch oder in der Schulgrammatik nachschlagen.

ENGLISCH MITTELSTUFE – Wir üben GRAMMATIK ist lernpsychologisch so aufgebaut:

1.
Hinführen und Nachdenken

Jedes Kapitel (= Groblernziel) beginnt mit allgemeinen Lernhilfen, d. h. Hinweisen auf typische Fehlerquellen.
Schwierige Vokabeln, auch solche aus unteren Klassen, sind alphabetisch aufgelistet und können notfalls abgerufen werden.

2.
Wiederholen und Üben

Die Aufgaben, die sich auf einen Rahmentext beziehen, behandeln zunächst einzelne, isolierte Schwierigkeiten. Es sind v. a. Fragen zum Text, Auswahl-Antwort-Aufgaben (= multiple-choice), Lückentexte, Umformungen und Übersetzungen. Themen, die seltener geprüft werden, sind mit * versehen und können bei Zeitmangel weggelassen werden.

3.
Selbständiges Arbeiten

Als nächster Lernschritt folgt eine Textaufgabe, ein Comprehension Test. Die Aufgaben sind vermischt und sollen das gesamte Kapitel abprüfen. Sie eignen sich auch als Hausaufgaben oder für Gruppenarbeit.

4.
Leistungskontrolle

Die Lösungsvorschläge zu den Comprehension Tests findet ihr im Beiheft. Es ist wichtig, daß ihr nachschaut, wie gut ihr selbständig gearbeitet habt.
Erst wenn ein Kapitel »sitzt«, solltet ihr das nächste Groblernziel (z. B. für die folgende Schulaufgabe oder Prüfung) in Angriff nehmen.

Viel Erfolg!

B) Die Zeiten (The Tenses)

Fehlerquellen:

1. **Beachtet die Signalwörter.**
   So verweist z. B. last week, 4j), auf Past Tense (saw), tomorrow, 6b), auf Future (will not rain) und ever since, 2c), auf Present Perfect (have been).
   Manche Signale sind im vorhergehenden oder folgenden Satz »versteckt«, z. B. 2b).
   Haltet insbesondere »Simple Present« und »Present Progressive« auseinander. Beachtet Signale wie every year, 3a), oder at the moment, 3g).
   Unterscheidet unbedingt zwischen »Past Tense« und »Present Perfect«, z. B. 4a) und 4c). Im Deutschen gibt es hier keinen vergleichbaren Unterschied.
2. **Verwechselt nicht »since« (= seit) und »for« (= seit).**
   Richtig ist: since 10 o'clock / Monday / May / 1983 (Zeitpunkt!)
   for 10 minutes / 5 hours / 20 years (Zeitraum!)
3. **Verwechselt nicht »ago« (= vor) und »for« (= seit).**
   also: I saw him 2 days ago. — Ich habe ihn vor 2 Tagen gesehen.
   I haven't seen him for 2 days. — Ich habe ihn seit 2 Tagen nicht mehr gesehen.
4. **Beachtet beim Übersetzen diesen wichtigen Unterschied:**
   Wir sind (schon) seit 5 Uhr hier. — **Präsens im Deutschen!**
   We have been here since 5 o'clock. — **Present Perfect im Englischen!**

Schwierige Vokabeln:

advice	Rat, Ratschlag	glory	Ruhm
(to advise)	(raten)	human	menschlich
bald	kahl, ohne Haar	in spite of	trotz
damp	feucht, dunstig	lawyer	Rechtsanwalt
driving licence	Führerschein	(law)	(Recht, Gesetz)
driving test	Fahrprüfung	to look forward to	s. freuen auf
te express	ausdrücken	performance	Vorstellung
(expression)	(Ausdruck, Äußerung)	(to perform)	(aufführen)
to fatten	dick werden	to place sth. at s. o's. disposal	jmd. etw. zur Verfügung stellen
(fat)	(dick, beleibt)	valley	Tal
to gather	s. versammeln		

Lösungen:	**Lernhilfen:**

1.

Die fettgedruckten Wörter im Text sind Verben in verschiedenen Zeitformen. Wir wiederholen:

a) einfache Form (simple form)
Present (I stay)
Past (I stayed)
Present Perfect (I have stayed)
Past Perfect (I had stayed)
Future (I shall stay)
Future Perfect (I shall have stayed)
Conditional (I should stay)
Conditional Perfect oder **Past Conditional** (I should have stayed)

b) Verlaufsform (Progressive Form oder Continuous Form)
Present (I am staying)
Past (I was staying)
Present Perfect (I have been staying)
Past Perfect (I had been staying)
Future (I shall be staying)
Conditional (I should be staying)
Future Perfect (I shall have been staying)
Conditional Perfect (I should have been staying)

2.

a) is

b) packed; had;

left; went;

was

c) have lived;

I have been

London

One bright June morning, when I **was** nineteen, I **packed** all I **had** on to my back, **left** my native village, and **went** up to London looking for gold and glory. That **was** more than fifteen years ago, and I **have been** here ever since. I **shall** probably **stay** here for the rest of my life. Yet in spite of all that I still cannot think of myself as a Londoner, nor ever will, nor ever want to.

For fifteen years I **have lived** in the flats and rooms of this city. Yet when I **talk** of my home I still **think** of that damp, green valley where I **was brought** up. The boys I **went** to school with **have** long since **grown** and **fattened, got** married and **gone** bald, and they **would** probably **have to have** a good long look at me before they **would recognize** me if I **turned** up there again.

Of course, London **is** the greatest show on earth, for never **have** so many human characters **gathered** together in one place. Here, in a day, you can see the world. Stand at the entrance to a mainline railway station during the rush-hour, and you **see** every possible kind of human being hurrying past.

2.

Study the text and fill in the gaps. Mind the tenses.

a) London .... the greatest show on earth.

b) When I was nineteen, I .... all I .... on to my back, ... my native village, and .... up to London. That .... more than fifteen years ago.

c) For fifteen years I .... in the flats and rooms of this city. I .... here ever since.

d) shall stay (will stay)

Oft: **I will** stay, **we will** stay anstelle von: **I shall** stay, **we shall** stay!

e) would have;

turned up

3.

Kurze Wiederholung:
Die einfache Gegenwart (**Simple Present Tense**) beschreibt Tatsachen in der Gegenwart; Dinge, die gewohnheitsmäßig oder oft geschehen. **Signalwörter** sind z. B.: **often, always, every year, usually, on Sunday, . . .**

Die Verlaufsform der Gegenwart (**Present Progressive Form**) beschreibt Vorgänge, die gerade vor sich gehen (»verlaufen«). **Signalwörter** sind z. B.: **now, just, at the moment; look; listen, . . .**

a) stays

b) comes

c) visit

d) visit

e) travel

f) work

Frageform!

g) are . . . working

»just« zwischen Hilfsverb und Verb!

h) am just doing

Meist keine Verlaufsform bei: to belong to, to know, to like, to love, to own, to remember, to see (= sehen), to seem, to want, to wish, . . .!

i) remembers

j) owns

k) know

l) see

d) I .... here for the rest of my life.

e) They .... to have a good long look at me before they

recognized me if I .... there again.

3.

Simple Present Tense or Present Progressive?

a) The man .... (stay) in London <u>every year.</u>

b) His family .... (come) from a village near London.

c) Many tourists .... (visit) London every year.

d) If you .... (visit) London you will meet a lot of interesting people.

e) When you .... (travel) in London next year, don't forget to see the Tower.

f) Thousands of Londoners .... (work) in one of the large banks.

g) Where .... you .... (work) <u>at the moment</u>? – In a classroom or in your study?

h) I .... (just + do) an exercise on the use of tenses.

i) The man .... (remember) his native village.

j) He .... (own) a flat in Kensington.

k) Most visitors to London .... (know) a little English.

l) At a railway station you .... (see) fascinating people.

4.

Kurze Wiederholung:
Die Vergangenheit (**Past Tense**) bezeichnet Vorgänge, die **vergangen** und **abgeschlossen** sind. **Signalwörter** sind z. B.: **last week, last year, yesterday, a month ago, when?.**
Das Perfekt (**Present Perfect**) bezeichnet Vorgänge oder Zustände, die in der Vergangenheit begonnen haben, aber noch an die Gegenwart heranreichen. **Signalwörter** sind z. B.: **ever since, recently, just, up to now, so far, since** und **for** (nur bei Bezug zur Gegenwart!).

---

a) arrived

b) was brought up

c) has been

d) have lost

e) have just bought

f) have often been

g) were

h) did . . . return

Frageform!

i) have seen

j) saw

Eindeutige Zeitangabe der Vergangenheit!

k) turned

→ **33.** Zeitenfolge im if-Satz!

l) had

Wunsch (»ich hätte«)!

5.

Das Plusquamperfekt (**Past Perfect**) ist als **Vorvergangenheit** meist mit der Vergangenheit (**Past**) sinngemäß verbunden. Das Ereignis, das weiter zurückliegt, steht im **Past Perfect.**

a) had lived

b) had arrived

4.
Past Tense or Present Perfect Tense?

a) The man .... (arrive) in London fifteen years ago.

b) He .... (be brought up) in a damp, green valley.

c) He lives in London now. He .... (be) here for fifteen years.

d) I .... (lose) my map of London; now I can't find my hotel.

e) I .... (just + buy) a new hat. Do you like it?

f) Do you know London? I .... (be + often) there.

g) .... (be) you in London last year?

h) When .... you .... to Germany (return)?

i) I .... (see) the film before; it's a good film.

j) I .... (see) the film last week.

k) If the man .... (turn) up again in his village, his old friends probably would not recognize him at once.

l) I wish I .... (have) a flat in Kensington.

5.
Past Tense and Past Perfect:

a) The man .... (live) in a village for nineteen years before he went up to London.

b) After he .... (arrive) in London, the man tried to find a room or a flat.

c) had already begun

d) had

→ **86** Zeitenfolge in der indirekten Rede!

e) had known

→ **33** Zeitenfolge bei den if-Sätzen!

f) had taken

Wunsch (»ich hätte ...... befolgt«)!

6.

Möglichkeiten:
a) I will travel (**Signalwörter** für zukünftiges Geschehen sind z. B.: **tomorrow, next year; I hope, I expect, . . .**)
b) I am going to travel (nahe Zukunft, Absicht, Wahrscheinlichkeit)
c) I am leaving tonight (geplante Handlung in der nahen Zukunft bei to go, to arrive, to leave, . . .)
d) I shall be leaving (**Future Progressive Form**)

a) will stay

b) will not rain (won't rain), isn't going to rain

c) will get

d) shall (will); (I'll)

e) shall (will)

f) will cost

g) is going

h) is leaving

auch: leaves

i) will be flying (will fly)

will be waiting (will wait)

d) When I reached the theatre the performance ....

.... (already + begin).

d) The man said, »I have lived here for many years«.

He said that he .... lived there for many years.

e) I didn't believe that London is so interesting. If I ....

(know) it, I would have come earlier.

f) I wish now that I .... (take) your advice.

6.
Expressing the future

a) The man .... (stay) in London for the rest of his life.

b) The weather forecast says it .... (not rain) tomorrow.

c) You .... (get) wet if you go out without an umbrella.

d) I .... (be) eighteen years old in June.

e) I hope I .... (see) you tonight.

f) I am afraid that a visit to Stratford .... (cost) a lot of money.

g) My friend .... (go) to London on Tuesday.

h) The train from London .... (leave) at half past seven tonight.

i) This time tomorrow I .... (fly) to London. My friend

.... (wait) for me at Heathrow Airport.

7.

a) did you do — Das **Signalwort** ›yesterday‹ folgt erst in der Antwort!

did; has not done it yet.

will do

b) have attended (have been attending)
had been — Vorzeitigkeit beachten!

c) has been — **Signalwort**: during the . . .!

did not work

d) was reading — **Verlaufsform**, wenn eine Handlung noch andauert, während die andere **eintritt**!

e) finish — **Infinitiv** ohne to nach Hilfsverb »must«!

8.

a) Mr. Brown has been living (has lived) in London for many years. — **for** two years, six hours, . . . (**Zeitraum**)!

b) Mr. Brown visited the Tower last Sunday.

c) I have not seen Mr. Brown since Monday. — **since** Monday, last week, December, eight o'clock, . . . (**Zeitpunkt**)!

d) Mr. Brown was just playing the piano, when I entered the room.

7.

Choose the correct form (mixed exercise)

a) When (you do) .... your homework?

I (do) .... it yesterday. My sister (not yet + do) ....

.... it. She (do) .... it tomorrow.

b) I (attend) .... this school since 1975.

Before I came here I (be) .... at a primary school.

c) During the last two hours Tom (be) .... rather busy.

He (not work) .... very hard last week.

d) I (read) .... the newspaper when my friend entered the room.

e) We must .... this exercise now. (finish)

8.

Übersetze: (Beachte die Unterschiede zum Deutschen!)

a) Herr Brown wohnt (schon) viele Jahre in London.

....

b) Herr Brown hat letzten Sonntag den Tower besucht.

....

c) Ich habe Herrn Brown seit Montag nicht gesehen.

....

d) Herr Brown spielte gerade Klavier, als ich das Zimmer betrat.

....

Comprehension Test: A Letter from London

9.

Give the correct form of the verbs.

You (be) .... surprised (get) .... a letter from London. I (be) .... here for two weeks now. You (know) .... that an uncle of mine (live) .... here; he is a lawyer. Last year he (invite) .... me (spend) .... my holidays in England. My uncle (have) .... a car of his own, which he (place) .... at my disposal. Fortunately I (pass) .... my driving test a few months ago, and (get) .... my driving licence. Though I (already + do) .... a lot of sightseeing, there are a great many things I (not yet + see) .... I could not help smiling when my uncle (congratulate) .... me on my English. (you + remember) .... how our English teacher often (find) .... fault with my English? He suggested that I (write) .... to you in English. I (look forward) .... to seeing you again.

10.
Which of the translations is correct?

a) Mein Onkel lebt seit zehn Jahren in London.
- ☐ My uncle lives in London for ten years.
- ☐ My uncle lived in London for ten years.
- ☐ My uncle has lived in London for ten years.

b) Ich helfe meiner Tante jeden Tag bei der Hausarbeit.
- ☐ Every day I help my aunt with the housework.
- ☐ Every day I am helping my aunt with her housework.
- ☐ Every day I have helped my aunt with her housework.

c) Letzte Woche ging ich auch einkaufen für sie.
- ☐ Last week I have also gone shopping for her.
- ☐ Last week I also went shopping for her.
- ☐ Last week I was also going shopping for her.

d) Ich las gerade die ›Times‹, als mein Onkel nach Hause kam.
- ☐ I read the Times when my uncle came home.
- ☐ I was just reading the Times when my uncle came home.
- ☐ I had just read the Times when my uncle came home.

e) Nachdem ich eine Woche in London verbracht hatte, fuhr ich zwei Tage nach Dover.
- ☐ After I have spent a week in London I went to Dover for 2 days.
- ☐ After I had spent a week in London I went to Dover for two days.
- ☐ After I had spent a week in London I have gone to Dover for 2 days.

f) Als ich zum Bahnhof kam, fuhr der Zug gerade ab.
- ☐ When I reached the station, my train left.
- ☐ When I was reaching the station, my train was just leaving.
- ☐ When I reached the station, my train was just leaving.

g) Ich lerne schon seit 1976 Englisch.
- ☐ I learnt English since 1976.
- ☐ I learn English since 1976.
- ☐ I have been learning English since 1976.

11.

Fill in the correct tense of the verbs given in brackets:

a) I think I (go) .... to London again. I suppose my uncle (invite) .... me.

b) I have decided to go sightseeing this afternoon. I (see) .... the Tower and Big Ben. I (come) .... back before it gets dark. I (bring) .... a friend with me.

c) I think Jim (just + leave) .... London.
No, he (leave) .... the day before yesterday.

d) Susan (be) .... in London for two weeks; she is still there. Jack (be) .... in London for only one week; he is back in Germany now.

e) First Tom passed his driving test, then he (get) .... his driving licence. → When Tom (pass) .... his driving test, he (get) .... his driving licence.

f) Tom (have) .... a discussion with an English boy now. He (understand) .... every word. He (remember) .... all the words which he (learn) .... at school. He (be) .... perfect in a few years.

C) Hilfsverben (Auxiliaries)

Fehlerquellen:

1. **Beachtet die Signalwörter.**
   So verweist next week, 16g), auf Future, a few days ago, 16i), auf Past.
2. **Fehlende Zeiten und Formen müssen durch Ersatzformen (= Substitutes) ausgedrückt werden,** z. B.

– Ich werde kommen können.	I'll be able to come. (Future!)
– Ich hoffe kommen zu können.	I hope to be able to come. (Infinitive!)

3. **Unterscheidet »must not« (= nicht dürfen) und »need not« (= nicht müssen),** z. B. 15).
4. **Vergeßt nicht bei »ought to« das »to«,** z. B. 15e).
5. **Hilfsverben brauchen bei Frage oder Verneinung kein »do/does/did«,** z. B. 17).
   Falsch!!! He doesn't can come. (= Er kann nicht kommen.)
6. **Beachtet die Besonderheiten bei der Umformung von der direkten in die indirekte Rede.**
   → Kapitel **I**.

Schwierige Vokabeln:

to carry out	ausführen, durchführen	to involve	hineinziehen
discovery	Entdeckung	lecture	Vortrag, Vorlesung
(to discover)	(entdecken)	possible	möglich
to enable	befähigen	to replace	ersetzen
(able)	(fähig, tüchtig)	to satisfy	befriedigen
equivalent	gleichwertig, entsprechend	science	Wissenschaft, Naturwissenschaft
to extract	hier: ableiten	speech	Rede
factory	Fabrik	(to speak)	(reden, sprechen)
gift	Geschenk, Gabe	ungrateful	undankbar
invention	Erfindung	(grateful)	(dankbar)
(to invent)	(erfinden)	weapon [e]	Waffe

Lösungen:	Lernhilfen:
	12. **To have, to be, to do** können zur Bildung besonderer Formen oder Zeiten verwendet werden (I have gone, I am reading, I don't sleep, ...); man bezeichnet sie dann als Hilfsverben (**Auxiliary Verbs**). **Can/could, may/might, will/would, shall/should, ought to, used to, must, dare, need** sind **unvollständige** Hilfsverben (**Defective auxiliary verbs**). Wir beachten besonders: a) He can go. (kein ›s‹ bei he, she, it!)
13.	b) Can you come? I can't come. (kein ›do/does‹ in Frage bzw. Verneinung!)
a) may	c) I can speak French. (Infinitiv ohne ›to‹ muß folgen!)
b) will	d) Es fehlen Formen für den Infinitiv, die Partizipien und alle Zeiten außer Present und z. T. Past. Für
c) can	die fehlenden Formen müssen **sinnverwandte Verben = Ersatzverben**
d) must	**(Substitutes)** eingesetzt werden.
e) has to	
f) is to; be able	to be able = Ersatzform für den fehlenden Infinitiv!

Do Translating Machines Exist?

Electronic computers are the only machines with which it **may** one day be possible to translate one language into another. The great problem, however, is to write programmes, which **will** enable the computer to carry out the many logical processes involved in translating. Let us suppose that we have an English text to be translated into German, and it is in a form which the machine **can** read. First the machine **has to** »look up« each English word in its own electronic dictionary. Of course, the machine **can't** simply replace an English word by an equivalent German word. It **has** also **to** know something about grammar. If a machine **is to** make usable translations, the machine itself **must be able to** extract the meaning of the text. But machines which **can** translate speech are much further off; and a machine which **can** make a satisfying translation of Shakespeare's plays is unlikely ever to be built.

13.
Fill in the suitable word from the text:

a) It .... one day be possible to use a translating machine.

b) A programme .... enable the computer to carry out logical processes.

c) It is difficult to make a programme which the machine .... read.

d) A translating machine .... be able to understand the meaning of a text.

e) The translating machine .... know a lot about grammar.

f) If a machine .... make good translations it must ....

.... to extract the meaning of the text.

14.

a)

Darf ich . . .

b)

. . . ob er dürfte

c)

Könnte ich . . .

d)

Es wird vielleicht wieder geschehen

e)

. . . er könnte vielleicht

f)

Ich habe nicht können

g)

. . . konnte ich

Diese Übungen sollen die verschiedenen Bedeutungen der einzelnen **Auxiliaries** erhellen. Die Übersetzung ins Deutsche verdeutlicht die Unterschiede für Schüler unserer Leistungsstufe am besten.

may = dürfen (Erlaubnis)
= können, vielleicht sein (Möglichkeit)

might = dürfte (Erlaubnis)
= könnte, könnte vielleicht (Möglichkeit)

Zur Bildung des Present Perfect verwenden wir **to be able to**!

can = können (Fähigkeit oder Möglichkeit)
= können, dürfen (Erlaubnis)

could = konnte (Vergangenheit!)
= könnte (unter gewissen Voraussetzungen)

14.

Which German translation comes nearest in meaning?

a) **May** I take this book? – No, you may not.

☐ Darf ich . . .
☐ Soll ich . . .
☐ Werde ich . . .

b) Tom asked if he **might** go to the lecture on computers.

☐ . . . ob er sollte
☐ . . . ob er dürfte
☐ . . . ob er möchte

c) **Might** I talk to you for a few minutes, please?

☐ Kann ich . . .
☐ Könnte ich . . .
☐ Möchte ich . . .

d) It **may** happen again.

☐ Es darf wieder geschehen.
☐ Es wird vielleicht wieder geschehen.
☐ Es muß wieder geschehen.

e) I'm not sure about it, but he **might** pass his test.

☐ . . . er möchte
☐ . . . er könnte vielleicht
☐ . . . er dürfte

f) I **have** not **been able to** translate the text.

☐ Ich kann nicht.
☐ Ich habe nicht können.
☐ Ich bin nicht in der Lage.

g) When I was four years old, I **could** already swim.

☐ . . . könnte ich
☐ . . . konnte ich
☐ . . . durfte ich

h)

. . . könntest du

→ **33:** if-Sätze!

i)

. . . sollen wir tun

Shall I/Shall we = soll ich/sollen wir? (Frage in der 1. Person!)
I shall come/We shall come = ich werde kommen/wir werden kommen (heute meist **I/we will**!)

j)

Ich werde arbeiten

k)

Du solltest machen

You should go = du solltest gehen, du solltest eigentlich gehen (Verpflichtung!)
I should come if you asked me = ich würde kommen → **33**

l)

. . . wir sollten

→ **86:** indirekte Rede!

m)

Ich würde dir helfen

auch: I would help you . . .

n)

Wir sollten eigentlich kommen

ought to = sollte eigentlich (starke Verpflichtung)

h) If you tried, you **could** write a good programme.

☐ ... konntest du
☐ ... müßtest du
☐ ... könntest du

i) What **shall** we do with this computer?

☐ ... sollen wir tun
☐ ... werden wir tun
☐ ... sollten wir tun

j) I **shall** work with this programme for two more years.

☐ Ich soll arbeiten
☐ Ich werde arbeiten
☐ Ich sollte arbeiten

k) You **should** do what your teacher tells you.

☐ Du sollst machen
☐ Du solltest machen
☐ Du würdest machen

l) Our teacher said that we **should** work harder.

☐ ... wir würden
☐ ... wir sollten
☐ ... wir sollen

m) I **should** help you if you asked me to.

☐ Ich sollte dir helfen
☐ Ich soll dir helfen
☐ Ich würde dir helfen

n) We **ought to** come for lessons twice every week.

☐ Wir sollten eigentlich kommen
☐ Wir sollen kommen
☐ Wir dürfen kommen

15.

a) have to go	auch: have got to go; am obliged to go
b) are allowed to smoke	auch: are permitted to smoke
c) am able to finish	
d) was able to swim	
e) ought to	Beachte: ought **to**!
f) are perhaps good	auch: can be good
g) am allowed to go out	auch: am permitted to go out
h) are not allowed to leave	auch: are not permitted to leave **must not** = nicht dürfen!
i) don't have to go; have to	**need not** = nicht zu brauchen, nicht müssen!
j) are we to do	Beachte: What are we **to** do = Was sollen wir tun?

16.

Wir suchen geeignete ›substitutes‹!

a) will be able	Futur für **can**!
b) be able	Infinitiv für **can**!
c) was able to	auch: could (Past Tense!)
d) should	›sollte‹! → **88**: indirekte Rede!

15.
Find a suitable substitute:

a) I (**must** go) .... to the doctor today.

b) You (**may** smoke) .... in this office.

c) I (**can** finish) .... this programme without help.

d) I (**could** swim) .... when I was only five years old.

e) We (**should** pay) .... the money for the computer.

f) Translating machines (**may** be good) ....

g) I (**may** go out) .... tonight.

h) We (**mustn't** leave) .... the room.

i) You (**needn't** go) .... home yet, but I (**must**) ....

j) What (**shall** we do) ....?

16.
Complete. Mind the forms of the auxiliaries:

a) A computer **can** translate easy texts into another language.

In the future a computer .... to translate difficult texts.

b) I hope I **can** do the work myself.

I hope to .... to do the work myself.

c) I **can** open the door.

I had a key, so I .... open the door.

d) **Shall** I ask the computer?

The translator asked if he .... ask the computer.

e)

would — ›würde‹! → **86:** indirekte Rede!

f)

might — → **88:** indirekte Rede!

g)

will be allowed — auch: will be permitted (dürfen)
Signalwort: next week!

h)

had to

will have to — auch: will be obliged to

i)

were not allowed to — auch: were not permitted to (durften nicht!)

17.

Wenn ein **Auxiliary** vorhanden ist, brauchen wir bei der Frage und Verneinung nicht mehr **do/does/did!**
Beachte: I must not = ich darf nicht
I need not = ich muß nicht

a) It is not easy . . . (It isn't)

b) The computer does not write (doesn't write)

c) A computer need not know — auch: . . . doesn't have to know

d) The machine doesn't have to write — auch: needn't write (kein **to**!)

e) Pupils must not use . . . — Sinngemäß: dürfen nicht!

e) I **shall** translate the text into German.

The interpreter said that he .... translate the text.

f) **May** I become a computer operator?

Tom asked his father if he .... become a computer operator.

g) We **may** visit the factory. The manager doesn't object.

We .... to visit the factory next week.

h) The specialist **must** repair the computer.

Yesterday the specialist .... repair the computer.

He .... repair the computer next week.

i) Visitors **must not** enter the room.

A few days ago visitors .... enter the room.

17.

Form the negative with »NOT«:

a) It **is** easy to construct computers.

....

b) The computer **writes** the programmes.

....

c) A computer **must** know all words.

....

d) The machine **has to** write texts.

....

e) Pupils **must** use translating machines in tests.

....

f)

Computers cannot write

auch: can't

g)

We didn't visit . . .

h)

I haven't heard of computers

18.

Wir üben hier besonders schwierige Formen!

a) Die Firma kann jetzt, aber nicht nächstes Jahr einen neuen Computer bezahlen.

b) Die Firma konnte . . . bezahlen.

c) Die Firma hat seit einiger Zeit . . . bezahlen können.

auch: kann schon seit . . . bezahlen.

d) Die Firma wird . . . bezahlen können.

e) Die Firma hätte . . . bezahlen können, wenn ein Bedarf vorhanden gewesen wäre.

f) Der Direktor soll nicht bei der Arbeit gestört werden.

g) Die Firma soll sehr modern sein.

He **is said to** be = er **soll** sein, er **ist angeblich**

f) Computers **can** write poems.

....

g) We **visited** a factory where computers are used.

....

h) I **have heard** of computers which can be used at school.

....

18.

Translate into German:

a) The firm **is able to** finance a new computer just now, but not next year.

....

b) The firm **was able to** finance the computer.

....

c) The firm **has been able to** finance new computers for some time.

....

d) The firm **will be able to** finance a new computer every year.

....

e) The firm **would have been able to** finance a computer if there had been a demand.

....

....

f) The manager **is** not **to be** disturbed during his work.

....

g) The firm **is said to be** very modern.

....

Comprehension Test: Atomic Energy

19.

Choose the correct form:

History shows how man always .... (is to, has to, has) choose between making the right or wrong use of science. This .... (was, has, had) never been more true than in our time, in which amazing discoveries and inventions have been made and are .... (having, being) made. It .... (should be, would be, were) ungrateful not to recognize how great the gifts are which science has brought to mankind. But the gifts of science .... (can, are able to, can't) be misused. It is this twofold use of science that .... (has, is, has to) raised the question: Is it right to discover or invent something that .... (must, can, may) be used for the destruction of us all? You know, of course, that I .... (have, am) thinking of the atomic bomb. At present the development is mainly directed towards the production of weapons designed to wipe out large parts of mankind. Is it right, therefore, to continue work which .... (may, must, shall) lead to such an end? I do not know, but I want to think it over.

(Cyril Garbett: Archbishop of York)

20.
Use a simple auxiliary for the expression in bold print:

a) Many people **are unable to** understand the dangers of atomic energy.

....

b) We **are** not **allowed to** misuse the gifts of science.

....

c) We **are obliged to** keep to strict safety rules.

....

d) Where **are** we **to** build atomic power stations?

....

e) **Are** you **able to** understand what the Archbishop of York meant?

....

f) We **don't have to** waste energy.

....

21.
Mind the tense!

a) We must save energy.

In the years to come we .... more energy.

b) I cannot understand the problem.

.... the problem, when I first read about it.

c) This work must be done.

This work .... when we opened the firm last year.

d) This work may lead to a terrible end.

The archbishop said that ....

22.
Change the sentences into the negative.

a) People **worked** less in the past.

....

b) We **ought to** forget the dangers of atomic energy.

....

c) I **know** all about atomic power stations.

....

d) We **may** stay in this part of the factory. It is forbidden.

....

e) We **can** learn all about physics in four years at school.

....

23.
Translate into German

a) We should think Cyril Garbett's words over.

....

b) What are we to do now?

....

c) What have you got to do here?

....

d) I'm sure we could save a lot of money.

....

e) They could have saved a lot of money if they had been more careful.

....

D) Aktiv – Passiv (Active – Passive)

Fehlerquellen:

1. **Beachtet auch hier die Signalwörter für bestimmte Zeiten.**
   z. B. at the moment, 28a), verlangt Present Progressive
   in the 21st century, 26g), verlangt Future
2. **Bei Satzumformungen vom Aktiv ins Passiv (oder umgekehrt), muß die Zeitstufe gleichbleiben.**
   Also: The government has promised . . . = Present Perfect Active
   They have been promised . . . = Present Perfect Passive; 27a)
3. **Wendet die passive Form des Infinitivs richtig an.**
   z. B. Energy must be saved.
   = Energie muß gespart werden. 27f)
4. **Oft müßt ihr ein geeignetes Subjekt finden, wenn ihr Passivsätze ins Aktiv verwandelt.**
   z. B. we, you, they (= man), people; 28d)
5. **Auch im Passiv sind Präpositionen eng mit ihrem Verb verbunden.**
   z. B. . . . nobody has dreamt of . . . = Active
   . . . has never been dreamt of . . . = Passive; 27e)

Schwierige Vokabeln:

amount	Menge, Betrag
area	Gebiet
to develop	sich entwickeln
(development)	(Entwicklung)
distant	entfernt
(distance)	(Entfernung)
efficient	tüchtig, leistungsfähig
to handle	umgehen mit
hydrogen	Wasserstoff
labour	Arbeit, Arbeitskräfte
to make use of	Gebrauch machen von, benutzen
muscle ['mʌsl]	Muskel
oxygen	Sauerstoff
plough [plaʊ]	Pflug
power station	Kraftwerk
recently	kürzlich, vor kurzem
to replace	ersetzen
resources	Bodenschätze
to run short of	knapp werden
to save	sparen
to solve	lösen
source of energy	Energiequelle
to split	spalten
to transmit	übermitteln
to use up	aufbrauchen
waterwheel	Wasserrad
windmill	Windmühle
wire	Draht

Lösungen:	Lernhilfen:
	24. **Grundmuster:** Animals pulled **ploughs.** **Ploughs** were pulled by animals. a) **Objekt** des Aktivsatzes (ploughs) wird **Subjekt** im Passivsatz. b) Die **Zeiten** müssen bei der Umwandlung gleichbleiben: They pulled = Past Tense They were pulled = Past Tense c) Bei der Umwandlung vom **Passiv** zum **Aktiv** muß oft ein sinnvolles **Subjekt,** z. B. they, people, you, . . . gefunden werden.
25. a) right b) wrong c) wrong d) right	
26.	Wiederhole die Bildung der Passivformen im Schulbuch!
a) is wasted	
b) are being built	to build, built, **built**
c) was done	to do, did, **done** (Wir brauchen die »3. Form« des Verbs, das »past participle«!)

Energy

For thousands of years people got all the energy they needed from the food they ate. All the work **was done** with their own muscles. Even today in large areas of the world, in such countries as China and India, most of the work **is** still **done** by human labour. Very soon, however, men learnt to use animals for the harder jobs, such as pulling ploughs or pumping water. Later, men began to build windmills and waterwheels that could take energy from the wind or from falling water. Today the place of the wooden waterwheels **has been taken** by the more efficient water turbines of the power stations which transform the energy of falling water into electrical energy that **can be transmitted** by wires to distant factories and cities.

25.
Right or wrong?

	R	W
a) People did all the work with their own muscles.	☐	☐
b) Wooden waterwheels have taken the place of turbines.	☐	☐
c) In India most of the work is done by machines.	☐	☐
d) Distant factories can be supplied by electrical energy.	☐	☐

26.
Form the passive in all tenses:

a) Simple Present Tense
A lot of energy .... (waste) nowadays.

b) Present Progressive Tense
More atomic power stations .... (build) every year.

c) Simple Past Tense
All the work .... (do) by people at that time.

d)
was being pumped

Beachte: Im Passiv gibt es nur zwei Verlaufsformen:
Present Continuous und Past Continuous!

e)
have been replaced

f)
had been done

g)
will be needed

h)
will have been built

i)
would be used

j)
would have been built

27.

a) The workers have been promised higher wages by the government.

auch: Higher wages have been promised to the workers. (2 Objekte!)

b) India is offered atomic power stations by America.

2 Objekte! → **Schulbuch**

c) All the work was left to the poor.

d) Past Progressive
Water .... (pump) into the fields for months in the summer.

e) Present Perfect
Waterwheels .... (replace) by turbines.

f) Past Perfect
Everything .... (do) quickly to provide enough energy.

g) Future Tense
More and more energy .... (need) in the 21st century.

h) Future Perfect
Many atomic power stations .... (build) by the year 2000.

i) Conditional
The windmills .... (use) all the time if they worked more effectively.

j) Conditional Perfect
More water turbines .... (build) years ago, if there had been enough water.

27.

Put the following sentences into the passive voice:

a) The government has promised the workers higher wages.

....

b) America offers India atomic power stations.

....

c) They left all the work to the poor.

....

d) Atomic power is made use of by many nations.

Präposition ›**of**‹ eng mit dem Verb verbunden!

e) Using sunlight for heating has never been dreamt of.

Objekt ›by nobody‹ fällt weg!

f) More energy must be saved.

Infinitiv Passiv!
(. . . muß gespart werden)

g) Nuclear energy ought to be handled with greater care in the future.

Infinitiv Passiv!

h) Power stations are being built in China.

Verlaufsform im Passiv nur in **Present Tense . . .**

i) When we were there, the power station was being repaired.

. . . und **Past Tense**!

28.

Beachte: Die Zeitform bleibt gleich!

a) Many nations are building atomic power stations at the moment.

b) Windmills could take energy from the wind in a few years' time.

c) If they find more uranium, they will build more power stations.

Beachte: Bei Umwandlung sinnvolles **Subjekt** suchen!

d) We must not waste energy.

auch: People . . .

e) Water turbines have replaced waterwheels.

d) Many nations make use of atomic power.

....

e) Nobody has ever dreamt of using sunlight for heating.

....

f) We must save more energy.

....

g) They ought to handle nuclear energy with greater care in the future.

....

h) They are building power stations in China.

....

i) When we were there, they were repairing the power station.

....

28.

Put the following sentences into the active voice:

a) Atomic power stations are being built by many nations at the moment.

....

b) Energy could be taken from the wind by windmills in a few years' time.

....

c) If more uranium is found, more power stations will be built.

....

d) Energy must not be wasted.

....

e) Waterwheels have been replaced by water turbines.

....

Comprehension Test: Energy (2)

Most of the energy now used by the people in the leading nations comes from oil, gas or coal. Nowadays the modern industries, households, cars, ships and aeroplanes need so much energy that many people fear that all these natural resources will be used up in a few years' time. Fortunately scientists have found a new source of energy: atomic energy. When uranium atoms are split, they release large quantities of heat energy. At present scientists are already working on a new kind of atomic energy using hydrogen which is less dangerous and even cheaper than the radioactive and very expensive uranium. The amount of hydrogen on our Earth is enormous because seawater is composed of hydrogen and oxygen. Thus in the near future men will have plenty of cheap energy at their disposal. More energy means more goods, more food and a higher standard of living for all mankind.

29.
Answer the following questions in the passive:

a) Who has found a new source of energy?

....

b) What releases large quantities of energy?

....

c) When will we use up the natural resources?

....

30.
Choose the correct answer:

a) If man doesn't find new sources of energy, the natural resources

.... in a few years' time.

- [ ] will being used up
- [ ] will be using up
- [x] will be used up
- [ ] will use up

b) To achieve a higher standard of living, more energy ....

☐ needs ☒ is needed
☐ is being needed ☐ has been needed

c) Nowadays experiments with new energies ....

☐ will be made ☐ have been made
☐ are making ☒ are being made

31.

Turn into the passive voice:

a) People say that oil is better for heating than coal.

....

b) Uranium atoms release large quantities of energy.

....

c) In ten years' time scientists will have found a new way of getting atomic energy.

....

....

d) In the near future men will produce plenty of cheap energy.

....

e) Everybody ought to save energy.

....

f) People say that scientists are solving the problems of energy.

....

g) Has anyone ever thought about that problem?

....

h) Nobody would have thought about that problem if energy had not run short recently.

....

....

i) If everyone in our country turned down the heating a little, we could save 10 per cent of the oil.

....

....

32.

Put the following sentences into the active voice. (You may have to add a suitable subject):

a) Another step has been taken towards the development of new sources of energy.

....

....

b) New ways of using atomic energy can be developed by scientists.

....

c) Most of the energy used by the leading nations must be saved before all the natural resources are used up.

....

....

d) Have these possibilities already been tested?

....

E) Konditionalsätze (Conditional Clauses; Bedingungssätze)

Fehlerquellen:

1. **Die Zeitformen im Hauptsatz (= Main Clause) und Nebensatz (= if-Clause) müssen sinngemäß zusammenpassen.**
   Wiederholt bitte das Grundmuster in Übung **33**.
   Beachtet, daß auch andere »Zeitkombinationen« sinnvoll sein können.
   z. B. If I were (= Past) you, I wouldn't have done it. (= Conditional Perfect)
2. **Verwendet in »echten« Bedingungssätzen kein »would«.**
   z. B. They could help you if you asked them. (Nicht!!!! would ask)
   = Sie könnten dir helfen, wenn du sie fragen würdest.
   Laß dich nicht vom Deutschen her verwirren!
3. **In Wunschsätzen und bei höflichen Bitten dagegen können »would/could/should« im if-Satz stehen.**
   Beachte die andere Bedeutung!
   z. B. We'd be glad if you would answer soon.
   = Wir würden uns freuen, wenn Sie bald antworten wollten.

Schwierige Vokabeln:

accommodation	Unterkunft	picturesque	malerisch
accustomed to	gewohnt an	(picture)	(Bild)
(custom)	(Gewohnheit)	pleasure	Vergnügen
choice	Auswahl	to provide	vorsehen, zur Verfügung stellen
(to choose)	(wählen)		
competition	Wettbewerb, Konkurrenz	to queue	sich anstellen, Schlange stehen
grateful	dankbar		
habit	Gewohnheit	to rent	vermieten
to hesitate	zögern	to save	sparen
in advance	im voraus	scenery	Landschaft
journey	Reise	seaside resort	Seebad
to make up one's mind	sich entschließen	sights	Sehenswürdigkeiten
		space	Raum
necessity	Notwendigkeit	variety	Vielfalt
(necessary)	(notwendig)		

Lösungen:	**Lernhilfen:**
	33. **Kurze Wiederholung:** **Zeitenfolge** im Regelfall (entscheidend ist immer der Sinnzusammenhang!): He **will work** if he **is** at home. He **must work** hard if he **wants** to pass his exam. He **would work** if he **were (was)** at home. He **would have worked** if he **had been** at home.
34.	
	Ask your teacher if you **don't know** the answer. (Imperativ!)
a) will have to pay	
	I **would be** glad if you **would** listen. (Wunschsatz!)
b) intend	Einleitende **Konjunktionen** sind: if, unless (= if not), provided that, on condition that, in case . . .
35.	
a) travel b) will . . . visit c) go	Reise sehr wahrscheinlich!

Holidays in Britain

The holiday habits of the British are an interesting study for those who are less accustomed to queueing for so many of the pleasures and necessities of life. It is well-known that the Britons don't only queue up **if** they want to get on a bus or train; they also queue for the cinemas and theatres; outside the fish and chip shops on Friday but also on the road **if** they want to go to the seaside in their car on Sunday. **Provided that** you intend to get holiday accommodation, you will find that the competition is so great that you'll sometimes be obliged to book your holiday a year in advance. **If** you are keen on renting a flat or cottage in the more picturesque areas of the country, you'll have to pay a particularly high price.

34.

Which answer is correct according to the text?

a) If you are keen on renting a flat, you .... a high price.
would have to pay | will have had to pay
would have had to pay | will have to pay

b) Provided that you .... to get accommodation, you'll be obliged to book in advance.
intended | will intend
intend | had intended

35.

Complete the following sentences:

a) What will you do if you .... (to travel) to Britain in your next summer holidays?

b) If I travel to Britain I .... (to visit) Scotland.

c) Provided that I .... (to go) to Edinburgh, I will certainly see the castle.

d) had

e) would spend

f) were

Vorstellung, was wäre, wenn . . .!

oft auch: If I was . . ., if he was . . .

g) had been

h) would have gone shopping

i) had had the chance

Was wäre geschehen, wenn . . .!
Die Bedingung kann nicht erfüllt werden, da der Satz sich auf Vergangenes bezieht.

j) would lend

k) would buy, bought

l) would be glad

In **Wunschsätzen** oft ›would‹ im ›if-Satz‹!
Die »Wunschfrage« wäre z. B.: Would you lend me a book?

m) tell

n) ask

o) take

if + Present Tense kann mit dem **Imperativ** (Befehlsform) verbunden sein!

d) What would you do if you .... (to have) enough money?

e) If I had enough money I .... (to spend) the weekend in London.

f) If I .... (to be) in London now, I would try to get tickets for a musical.

g) What would you have done if you .... (to be) in London with us last summer?

h) If I had been in London with you last summer, I ....

.... (to go shopping) in Carnaby Street.

i) If I .... (to have the chance) of going on holiday, I would have travelled to Scotland.

j) I would be grateful if you .... (to lend) me a book about Britain.

k) We would be pleased if you .... (to buy) tickets for us.

l) I .... (to be glad) if you would come to Britain with us.

m) If you can't come with us, ... (to tell) us in time.

n) If you haven't got enough money, ... (to ask) your father for some.

o) Supposing a flight to London is too expensive, ... (to take) a train.

36.

a) were	auch: was
b) must book	Auxiliary »must« hier sinnvoll!
c) must be paid	Passiv!
want	
d) would you like to visit	Beachte: Fragestellung!
e) had	unless = if not!
f) Wouldn't you have been happy Would you not have been happy	
g) would show	Beachte: Wunschsatz!
h) would be delighted	
i) should save	Sinn entscheidet! auch: ought to save
j) could help, would help	je nach Sinnzusammenhang!
k) should go	oder: ought to go

36.

Use the correct tense:

a) If I .... (to be) you I would plan a tour through Wales.

b) If you want to get holiday accommodation, you .... (to book) in advance.

c) A particularly high price .... (must/pay) if you .... (to want) to go on holiday in August.

d) Which places ....(you/to like/to visit) if you happened to come to Wales?

e) I would not plan a tour through Britain, unless I .... (to have) enough time.

f) .... (you/not to be happy) if you had had the opportunity of flying to London?

g) My friend would be grateful if you .... (to show) him some slides.

h) I .... (to be delighted) if I could join your party.

i) You .... (to save) your pocket money if you want to go on holiday to Britain.

j) If you were lost in London, a policeman .... (to help) you.

k) If you happen to be in Liverpool, you really .... (go) to a football match at Anfield.

Comprehension Test: Holidays in Britain

If you had the choice, where would you like to spend your holidays in Britain? Would you like to stay in a hotel or guest house, would you prefer a caravan holiday or would you go camping? If you wanted to get away from the big seaside resorts, you could choose one of the small islands around Britain. They offer a great variety of scenery and local amusements. Some of the larger and better known are the Isle of Wight and the Isle of Man and of course the Orkneys and Shetlands in the North of Scotland. But if you really travel to Britain, you'll certainly visit London and Edinburgh. You'll be able to see all the famous sights and if you come in August the Edinburgh Festival will be held. There are so many places in Britain worth seeing that you'll travel through Britain many times if once you have started to visit it.

37.

Answer the following questions in complete sentences:

a) What could you do if you wanted to get away from the big seaside resorts?

....

....

b) Which cities will you see if you really travel to Britain?

....

....

c) What will take place in Edinburgh if you come in August?

....

....

38.

Choose the correct answer:

a) If Peter had a chance, he .... in a hotel.

had stayed	would have stayed
would stay	will stay

b) John would not have gone camping if he .... that it would rain.

knew	would know
had known	would have known

c) »Paul, if you come to London, ... and see the Tower.«

go	must go
will go	are going

d) »Unless you have seen Edinburgh, you .... that you know Scotland.«

won't be able to say	can say
will say	would be able to say

39.

In each of the if-clauses there is one mistake. Write your correction in the space provided:

a) If you would ask your father, he will allow you to come with us.

....

b) If I am you, I would inform myself about Britain.

....

c) If Bob would save his money, he could fly to Aberdeen.

....

d) If your father said ›yes‹, you must not hesitate to spend your holidays in the Isle of Wight.

....

40.

Complete the sentences. Use the expressions given in brackets:

a) If I had the choice I .... (like to spend) my holidays in Britain.

b) If you really travel to Britain, you .... (can see) all the famous sights.

c) You should ask your father if you .... (to want to fly) to London.

d) Sandra wouldn't have believed it if she .... (not to tell) that Edinburgh is the most beautiful city in Scotland.

41.

Complete the following dialogue using the right tense of the verbs in brackets:

Sheila: »Have you made up your mind yet, whether you ....

.... (to come) on holiday with us?«

Ian: »No, not yet, because my father .... only .... (to give) me the money for the journey if I .... (to pass) my exams this year.«

Sheila: »I think, you could easily succeed if you ....

(to learn) a little more. If I .... (to be) you, I ....

.... (to pay attention) at school.«

Ian: »And I .... (to be glad) if you ....

.... (not to remind) me of that all the time.«

F) Infinitiv (Infinitive, Grundform des Verbs)

Fehlerquellen:

1. **Beachtet, daß nach gewissen Verben nur der to-Infinitiv möglich ist.**
   z. B. They decided to build. 48a)
   Nach anderen Verben kann nur die -ing-Form (= Gerund) folgen.
   z. B. Would you mind coming again? 48c)
   Nach manchen Verben gibt es beide Möglichkeiten.
   z. B. Tom likes dancing. Tom likes to dance. 59)
   Diese Verben solltet ihr im Lehrbuch gründlich wiederholen!
2. **Erkennt die häufige Satzkonstruktion »Verb + Objekt + to-Infinitiv«. Beachtet den Unterschied zum deutschen Satzbau.**
   z. B. We want him to come.
   = Wir wollen, daß er kommt. 44)
3. **Haltet die Konstruktionen »Make + Objekt + Infinitiv« bzw. »Let + Objekt + Infinitiv« auseinander.**
   Also: The teacher makes the boys work hard.
   (Er läßt sie arbeiten; d. h. er veranlaßt es, daß sie arbeiten)
   Mr Brown lets his son drive his car.
   (Er läßt es zu, daß er den Wagen fährt)

Schwierige Vokabeln:

to advise	raten	prosperity	Wohlstand, Blüte
(the advice)	(Ratschlag)	to reread	nochmals durchlesen
authorities	Behörde	(to read)	(lesen)
to complain	beklagen	to run the risk	Gefahr laufen
consequently	folglich, deshalb	to settle down	sich niederlassen
to cope with	fertig werden mit	slowness	Langsamkeit, Schwerfälligkeit
efficient	tüchtig, leistungsfähig		
to erect	errichten	(slow)	(langsam)
to expect	erwarten	to solve	lösen
factory	Fabrik	undecided	unentschlossen
to get used to	sich gewöhnen an	(to decide)	(sich entscheiden)
to hesitate	zögern	value	Wert
impartial	unparteiisch, gerecht		
to persuade	überreden, überzeugen		

Lösungen:	**Lernhilfen:**

42.

Grundmuster:

The planners expect **the families to leave** London. **(Objekt + Infinitiv mit to)** → **44**

The architects ordered **the houses to be built. (Objekt + passiver Infinitiv mit to)** → **45**

It was the **best** thing **to do**. Mr. Brown was **the first to come. (Superlativ bzw. Zahlwort + Infinitiv mit to)** → **45**

It was difficult **for people to go** to work. **(Präposition + Substantiv + Infinitiv mit to)** → **46**

Many people didn't know **what to do. (Fragewort + Infinitiv mit to)** → **47**

43.

a) The planners expected some of the population of the capital to move to these new towns.

Objekt + Infinitiv mit to! → **44**

b) Twelve new towns have been built ... in the best area to be found. These were the last buildings to be put up in the new towns. They were the first to come.

Infinitiv mit to nach **Superlativen** bzw. **Zahlwörtern**! → **45**
hier: passiver Infinitiv!

New Towns and their Problems

Since the end of World War II, twelve new towns have been built in Britain, eight of them around London in the best area **to be found**. The planners expected some of the population of the capital **to move** to these new towns. The houses and factories, shops and schools, offices and churches, hospitals, cinemas and restaurants, all had to be built in the right place, so that there would be no factories without workers, no workers without jobs, no children without schools, no house-wives without shops and no family without a place to live in. However, there were problems which were not easy for the planners **to solve**. No family or firm in Britain could be forced to move to a new town, and many people thought they would find life too lonely away from their friends and neighbours. As a result, industrialists were slow to set up factories there. Consequently houses were sometimes finished before the factories, and workers had to travel a long way to work. Sometimes it was the other way round, and there were complaints about the slowness in building houses, shops and schools. Again, some of those who were the first **to come** didn't know how **to spend** their spare time. They missed dance-halls, cinemas etc.; for these were the last buildings **to be put up** in the new towns.

43.

Reread the text and arrange the infinitive structures in bold print according to the following examples:

a) The planners want **them to leave** London.

....

....

b) This was **the boldest plan** ever **to be put** forward.

....

....

c) There were problems which were not easy for the planners to solve.

Infinitiv mit to nach **Präpositionen** (for, on, with, without)! → **46**

d) Some of those didn't know how to spend their spare time.

Infinitiv mit to nach **Fragewörtern** (What, where, when, why, whether, how)! → **47**

44.

Die Konstruktion **Objekt + Infinitiv mit to** steht z. B. nach den Verben: to advise, to allow, to ask, to command, to expect, to force, to hate, to order, to permit, to want, to wish . . .
→ **Schulbuch**

a) The experts advised them to move to the new towns.
b) They invited them to study the plans.

c) Most parents wanted the children to leave the city.
d) Jennifer would have liked her friends to move as well.
e) They couldn't order her to leave her flat in London.
f) They considered him to be an expert.

45.

Infinitiv mit to nach **Superlativen** (the best, the most, the next) bzw. **Zahlwörtern** (the first, the last, the only thing)!

a) The Browns were the last family to leave London.

b) This was the first factory to start production.

c) It was difficult **for** the people **to settle** down there.

....

....

d) They were undecided about **when to leave** London.

....

44.

Complete these sentences in order to get the same infinitive construction as the following:

The architects expected **the families to leave** London.

a) The experts advised (they, move) .... to the new towns.

b) They invited (they, study) .... the plans.

c) Most parents wanted (the children, leave) .... the city.

d) Jennifer would have liked (her friends, move) .... as well.

e) They couldn't order (she, leave) .... her flat in London.

f) They considered (he, be) .... an expert.

45.

Replace the relative clauses by infinitive constructions:

a) The Browns were the last family who left London.

The Browns were the last family to ....

b) This was the first factory which started production.

....

c) This is the most comfortable flat to be found.

d) It was the strangest idea ever to be realised.

e) The next buildings to be erected are schools.

Passiver Infinitiv!

46.

Infinitiv mit to nach **Präposition + Substantiv** bzw. **Pronomen!**

a) The rent is too high for the family to pay.

b) It was very kind of you to show us round.

c) The schools are too far away for the children to walk there.

d) It was very thoughtless of the architects to forget playgrounds.

Beachte, wie die Sätze sinngemäß verbunden werden!

47.

Infinitiv mit to nach **Fragewörtern!**

a) They didn't know where to spend their free time.

c) This is the most comfortable flat which can be found.

....

d) It was the strangest idea which was ever realised.

....

e) The next buildings which will be erected are schools.

....

46.

Use the given prepositions and an infinitive construction to make one sentence: for – of – for – of

a) The rent is too high. The family cannot pay it.

....

b) You showed us round. It was very kind.

....

c) The schools are too far away. The children cannot walk there.

....

d) The architects forgot playgrounds. It was very thoughtless.

....

47.

Shorten the following sentences by using the infinitive after the question word:

a) The people didn't know <u>where they should spend</u> their free time.

They didn't know <u>where</u> ....

b) The planners showed them how to solve the problem.

c) The families were told when to move.

d) The newcomers didn't know what to do in the evenings.

e) Some old people don't know how to get used to their new surroundings.

48.

a) to build

b) leaving

c) losing

d) living

e) moving

f) to get

Nach einigen Verben kann im Englischen das **Gerund** oder der **Infinitiv** stehen! → **59**
Nach gewissen Verben steht nur der **Infinitiv** (z. B. to decide, to manage, to promise, to refuse, to want, to wish)!
Nach anderen Verben darf nur das **Gerund** verwendet werden (z. B. to admit, to avoid, cannot help, to dislike, to enjoy, to go on, to mind, to risk)! → **58**
→ **Schulbuch**

b) The planners showed them how they could solve the problem.

....

c) The families were told when they should move.

....

d) The newcomers didn't know what they should do in the evenings.

....

e) Some old people don't know how they can get used to their new surroundings.

....

48.

Infinitive or Gerund?

a) The government decided (build) twelve new towns.

....

b) Some people disliked (leave) London.

....

c) Others didn't mind (lose) their friends.

....

d) When they had settled in, many of them enjoyed (live) there.

....

e) Many families realised it was a good idea (move) out of the city.

....

f) Mr Brown had hoped (get) used to the new surroundings quickly.

....

Comprehension Test: Why go to School?

Have you ever considered why children go to school? We expect them to learn their own language, other languages, arithmetic, history, and all the other subjects which are often difficult for them to cope with. But why do they learn these things? Is this the best way to prepare them for life? We want our children to be prepared for the future when they will be grown-up and work for their own prosperity. For that reason there is more value in education than in just learning facts. In the end we go to school to learn how to learn, so that, when we have left school, we can continue to learn. A man who really knows how to learn will always be successful, because whenever he has to do something which he has never done before, he will rapidly teach himself to do it in the best way.

49.

Which of the following sentences has got the same structure as:

a) We expect them to learn languages.

☐ We send them to school in order to learn languages.
☒ The teacher tells him to do his homework carefully.
☐ It is valuable to learn languages.
☐ We go to school to learn how to learn.

b) It is difficult for them to cope with the problem.

☐ We want our children to be prepared for life.
☐ It is difficult to learn how to learn.
☐ We can continue to learn.
☒ It is not easy for him to learn Hebrew.

c) He really knows how to learn.

☐ It is never too late to start learning.
☐ I don't want to go to school any longer.
☒ The teacher tells them what to do.
☐ Is this the best way to prepare them for life?

50.
Finish the following sentences:

a) His parents want (he, go on) .... to university.

b) Most parents expect (their children, work) .... hard at school.

c) The teachers advise (we, to do exercises) ....

d) Mr. Brown permits (the boy, leave) .... earlier.

e) My friend has persuaded (I, take) .... Greek as an optional subject.

f) I can hardly believe (she, be) .... the best student.

g) Mr. Brown encouraged (Bill, try) .... again.

51.
Replace the infinitive constructions by relative clauses:

a) This is the best method to be thought of.

....

b) This is the most useful book on grammar to be bought.

....

c) Tom and Susan were the last students to leave the hall.

....

d) For Tom English is the most interesting subject to be chosen.

....

e) This was the worst play to be performed at our school.

....

52.

Shorten the following sentences by using the infinitive after the question word:

a) Children usually don't understand how they should work efficiently.

....

....

b) You must always tell them what they should do and how they should do it.

....

....

c) The teacher told Bob when he should do his homework.

....

d) The newcomers wanted to know where they should go to school.

....

53.

Combine the sentences by using the correct preposition and an infinitive construction:

a) The text is too difficult. The students cannot read it.

....

b) We must learn different structures. It is necessary.

....

c) He helped the old lady. It was very kind.

....

d) The suitcase was too heavy. The old lady could not carry it.

....

G) Gerund (-ing-Form)

Fehlerquellen:

1. **Beachtet, daß nach gewissen Verben nur die -ing-Form möglich ist.**
   z. B. Would you mind coming again? 48c)
   Nach bestimmten anderen Verben darfst du nur den to-Infinitiv verwenden.
   z. B. They decided to build. 48a)
   Nach manchen Verben gibt es beide Möglichkeiten. 59)
2. **Prägt euch die richtigen Präpositionen dieser Satzbaumuster ein:**
   – Substantiv + Präposition + -ing-Form 60)
   – Adjektiv + Präposition + -ing-Form 61)
   – Verb + Präposition + -ing-Form 62)
   Merkt euch ganz besonders interested in (= interessiert an) und to look forward to (= s. freuen auf).
3. **Haltet die folgenden Formen von »use« und »used« auseinander.**
   z. B. I'm used to getting up early. = Ich bin es gewöhnt, früh aufzustehen.
   Tom used to smoke. = Tom hat früher geraucht.
   You may use your books. = Ihr dürft eure Bücher benutzen.
4. **Beachtet, daß eine wörtliche Übersetzung selten möglich ist.**
   z. B. I'm fond of smoking. = Ich rauche gern.
   Do you mind my smoking? = Hast du etwas dagegen, wenn ich rauche?
   On entering the room . . . = Beim Betreten des Zimmers . . .

Schwierige Vokabeln:

absorbed in	vertieft in	to dread [e]	fürchten
advisable	ratsam	eventful	ereignisreich
(to advise)	(raten)	(event)	(Ereignis)
to avoid	vermeiden	to feel like doing	Lust haben, etwas zu tun
beauty	Schönheit	to glide	gleiten
(beautiful)	(schön)	invader	Eindringling, Angreifer
to conquer	erobern	(to invade)	(eindringen)
to cover	(Entfernung) zurücklegen	narrow	eng, schmal
to delay	verzögern	to prevent from	hindern an
(the delay)	Verzögerung	smooth	glatt, ruhig
to deny	leugnen, abstreiten		

Lösungen:	Lernhilfen:
	54. **Kurze Wiederholung:** Das Gerund wird im Englischen häufig wie folgt verwendet: **Flying** is fun. **(Subjekt) → 56** He continued **reading**. **(Objekt) → 58** He is absorbed in **reading**. **(nach Präpositionen) → 60, 61, 62, 63**
55.	Wir wiederholen einige Anwendungsmöglichkeiten des Gerunds:
a) from conquering	Verb + Präposition + Gerund (prevent + from + conquering) **→ 62**
b) Flying; of going	Gerund als Subjekt (Flying) **→ 56** Substantiv + Präposition + Gerund (way + of + going) **→ 60**
c) in reading	Adjektiv + Präposition + Gerund (absorbed + in + reading) **→ 61**
d) spending	Gerund als Objekt! **→ 58**

Going to Britain

As Britain is an island the classical way to go to England is by ship. All the invaders in Britain's eventful history had to cross a narrow strip of sea which could not prevent them from conquering the country. For the modern traveller from the Continent there is still something strangely exciting about approaching the island, no matter whether he is shaken up and down in a heavy Channel sea or glides smoothly over gentle waves towards the white cliffs of Dover.

For people who prefer a shorter and more comfortable passage there is another way of going to Britain – that is flying. Whereas the journey from Munich to London by train and boat takes at least 18 hours, a passenger can cover the same distance in as little as one and a half hours if he flies. Therefore buying a flight ticket is advisable if you don't mind spending more money. In addition the air passenger, too, has the thrilling experience of approaching an island. Provided he is not absorbed in reading a paper, he will get a fine bird's eye view of first the Continent, then the Channel, and finally the silver coast and England itself.

55.

Complete the following sentences according to the text:

a) The narrow strip of sea could not prevent the invaders ....

.... the country.

b) .... is another way .... to Britain.

c) Someone who is not absorbed .... a paper will get a fine bird's eye view of the Channel.

d) Do you mind .... more money?

56.

a) Going to Britain is a valuable experience.

b) Speaking English is a great help.

c) Speaking English well is difficult.

d) Noticing the differences between Germany and England is interesting.

e) Being able to drive a car is very useful.

57.

Das Gerund steht auch nach folgenden Ausdrücken:
there is no . . .
it is no good . . .
it is no use . . .
it is (not) worth while . . .
what about . . .?
how about . . .?

a) There is no denying the fact that flying is more comfortable than going by train.

b) Is London really worth seeing?

56.

Transform the following sentences by changing the verbs in bold print into gerunds and using them as subjects:

a) It's a valuable experience **to go** to Britain.

....

b) It's a great help **to speak** English.

....

c) It's difficult **to speak** English well.

....

d) It's interesting **to notice** the differences between Germany and England.

....

e) It's very useful **to be** able to drive a car.

....

57.

Complete the following sentences by using the gerund:

a) There is no (to deny) the fact that (to fly) is more comfortable than (to go) by train.

....

....

b) Is London really worth (to see)?

....

c) It is no good buying a flight ticket; . . .

it is no good = es hat keinen Zweck

d) It is worth while going to Britain.

it is worth while = es lohnt sich

e) What about taking a charter plane?

f) How about staying another week?

= wie wäre es, wenn . . .?

58.

Muster:
Would you **mind opening** the door?
Nach bestimmten Verben folgt im Englischen das Gerund. → **48**

a) being

b) putting off

c) packing

d) carrying

e) going

f) flying

g) telling

h) smiling

Beachte: He stopped to tell me something about Britain. (Er hielt an, um mir etwas über Großbritannien zu erzählen!)
Stop telling me about London. (Hör damit auf, mir von London zu erzählen!)

c) It is no good (to buy) a flight ticket; the pilots are on strike.

....

d) It is worth while (to go) to Britain.

....

e) What about (to take) a charter plane?

....

f) How about (to stay) another week?

....

58.

Use a suitable gerund from the following list to complete the sentences:

being – flying – carrying – going – packing – putting off – smiling – telling

a) Excuse my .... late; I couldn't find my ticket.

b) I don't mind your .... the departure.

c) I have just finished .... my suitcase.

d) Would you mind .... it? It is too heavy for me.

e) Why don't you go by train? – I dislike .... by train.

f) I enjoy .... in an aeroplane.

g) Stop .... me about your visit to Britain.

h) I could not help .... when the air hostess offered me a drink.

59.

a) After the invaders had crossed the Channel they started conquering the island.

b) I intend going to Britain next summer.

c) Therefore I continue preparing myself for the trip.

d) I hate being shaken up and down in a heavy sea.

e) That is why I prefer flying.

f) I also hate sitting in the train for hours and hours.

g) I dread travelling alone at night.

Kurze Wiederholung:
He **begins to plan** his trip to Britain.
He **begins planning** his trip to Britain.
Nach einigen Verben kann im Englischen das **Gerund** oder der **Infinitiv** stehen. → **48**

Beachte den Unterschied:*
I like **to travel** to England **this summer.**
I like **travelling.** – It is my hobby.

Bei Verben wie to like, to love, to prefer, to fear drückt das **Gerund** oft etwas **Allgemeines** aus, während der **Infinitiv** einen Einzelfall schildert.

60.

a) for being angry

b) in studying foreign languages

Das Gerund steht nach **Substantiven**, die eng mit einer **Präposition** verbunden sind (z. B. reason for)!

59.
Replace the infinitive by the gerund:

a) After the invaders had crossed the Channel they started <u>to conquer</u> the island.

....

....

b) I intend to go to Britain next summer.

....

c) Therefore I continue to prepare myself for the trip.

....

d) I hate to be shaken up and down in a heavy sea.

....

e) That is why I prefer to fly.

....

f) I also hate to sit in the train for hours and hours.

....

g) I dread to travel alone at night.

....

60.
Rewrite the sentences:

a) One of the passengers <u>is angry</u>.

There is no reason ....

b) The captain studies foreign languages.

The captain takes great interest ....

c) of starting the plane.

d) in looking after the passengers.

Passiv!

e) for flying to Australia

f) of going to Britain

g) of visiting it

61.

Gerund nach **Adjektiven,** die fest mit einer **Präposition** verbunden sind (z. B. fond of)!

a) in reading newspapers

b) in looking after the passengers

c) of answering all the questions

d) to travelling by plane

e) of spending some days in Britain

f) in travelling to Britain

c) The pilot is just about to start the plane.

He is on the point ....

d) The air-hostesses look after the passengers.

They have great experience ....

e) Many people like to fly to Australia.

Winter is the best time ....

f) Have you ever gone to Britain?

Have you ever had the chance ....

g) It is beautiful to visit Scotland in autumn.

Is there any possibility .... then?

61.

Rewrite the sentences by using the words given below. Mind the correct preposition.

a) Some passengers <u>read newspapers</u>.

They were absorbed ....

b) The stewardess looked after the passengers.

She was engaged ....

c) She answered all the questions.

She was not tired ....

d) Many businessmen travel by plane.

They are used ....

e) I spend some days in Britain.

I am fond ....

f) Would you also like to travel to Britain?

Are you also interested ....?

62.

Gerund nach **Verben**, die eng mit einer **Präposition** verbunden sind (z. B. to apologize for)!
Überlegen Sie, mit welchem Satzteil Sie sinngemäß beginnen müssen!

a) The flight captain apologized for being late.

b) The passengers complained of (about) not being told about the delay.

c) They were looking forward to seeing their relatives soon.

d) The stewardess was blamed for not serving any drinks.

e) In the end the captain succeeded in being punctual.

63.

Konstruktion: **Präposition + Gerund**! (im Deutschen meist Nebensatz!)

a) Instead of flying to England he went by boat.

b) The tourist prepared himself for his stay in Britain by studying a map of London.

c) One of the passengers left without saying good-bye.

d) He entered the house without saying a word.

62.

Combine the two parts of the sentence by using a gerund and the correct preposition:

a) The flight captain apologized / he was late

....

b) They were not told about the delay / the passengers complained

....

c) They were looking forward / they see their relatives soon

....

d) The stewardess was blamed / she didn't serve any drinks

....

e) In the end the captain succeeded / he was punctual

....

63.

Form one sentence out of each pair of sentences using gerunds with the given preposition:

a) He did not fly to England. He went by boat. (instead of)

....

b) The tourist prepared himself for his stay in Britain. He was studying a map of London. (by)

....

c) One of the passengers left. He didn't say good-bye. (without)

....

d) He entered the house. He didn't say a word. (without)

....

Comprehension Test: A Slight Delay

I had spent my last day in London doing some shopping. Among other things I had intended buying an alarm clock. After travelling in a crowded bus I was glad to be sitting in the plane at last and was looking forward to seeing my family again. In a few minutes now we would be up in the sky on our flight to Berlin. Ten minutes later, instead of enjoying the beauty of the evening sky, I was sitting in a room with two police officers at my side. There was no denying the fact that I felt quite uncomfortable. On the table was one of my suitcases. The officers asked me to show them my passport, opened the suitcase and spread out its contents on the table. When I placed the alarm-clock on the table, they looked at each other. Hearing the clock ticking, I suddenly understood and could not help smiling. Someone must have heard the ticking noise coming out of my suitcase and thought there was a time bomb hidden in it. The officers apologised for examining my luggage and I could finally enjoy travelling home.

64.

Which of the following sentences has got the same structure?

»They apologised for examining my luggage«

☐ He had intended buying an alarm clock.
☒ He was looking forward to seeing his family.
☐ The tourist was showing his passport to them.
☐ Someone must have heard the ticking noise.

»There is no denying the fact«

☐ He could not help smiling.
☐ He is not going to Scotland.
☐ Having examined the case the officers let him go.
☐ It is worth while visiting London.

»He could not help smiling.«

☒ He enjoyed travelling home.
☐ Instead of enjoying the flight he was arrested.
☐ The officers arresting him were very polite.
☐ He had done some shopping.

65.
Translate into German:

a) I had spent my last day in London doing some shopping.

....

b) I was looking forward to seeing my family again.

....

c) There was no denying the fact that I felt quite uncomfortable.

....

d) The officers apologised for examining my luggage.

....

66.
Combine the two parts of the sentence by using a gerund and the correct preposition if necessary:

a) He was very keen / to get back to Berlin

....

b) He had no chance / to explain the ticking in the case

....

c) He opened the suitcase / he didn't object to it

....

d) At last the police officers succeeded / they found something

....

e) The tourist smiled / he couldn't help it

....

67.

Infinitive or gerund? In which sentences are both forms possible?

a) On my last day in London I felt like (go) .... shopping.
b) I couldn't bear (visit) .... one sight after the other.
c) Therefore I tried to avoid (stay) .... with the group.
d) I managed (disappear) .... without

(be) .... seen and then decided (walk) ....

....................down Oxford Street.

e) I enjoyed (look) .... into the shop-windows

and (compare) .... the prices.

f) Then I began (think over) .... what presents I could buy.

68.

Rewrite these sentences following the suggestion below; add the correct preposition from the list below: by – in case of – without

a) He must make up for lost time. He must hurry to the plane.

He must make up for lost time .... to the plane.
b) The policemen must arrest him and not cause a sensation.

The policemen must arrest him .... a sensation.
c) He will have to stay over night if he misses his plane.

He will have to stay over night .... his plane.

H) Partizipsätze (Participial Clauses)

Fehlerquellen:

1. **Haltet aktives und passives Partizip auseinander.**
   z. B. The policeman standing . . . comes from London.
   = The policeman who is standing . . . (. . ., der steht: Aktiv!)

   The car driven by the woman . . .
   = The car that was driven . . . (. . ., der gefahren wurde: Passiv!)
2. **Beachtet, daß die Zeiten von Haupt- und Nebensatz übereinstimmen müssen, wenn ihr einen Partizipsatz in einen Nebensatz umformt. Das Partizip kann sich ja auf verschiedene Zeiten beziehen.**
   z. B. Here's the girl wearing a blue pullover.
   → Here's the girl who is wearing . . . (Present: Here is!)
   Bill talked to the girl sitting in the garden.
   → Bill talked to the girl who was sitting . . . (Past: talked!) 77)
3. **Bei der Satzverkürzung muß klar bleiben, wer oder was gemeint ist.**
   z. B. When Mrs Brown drove into town, she noticed a dog.
   → When driving into town, Mrs Brown noticed a dog.
4. **Oft entscheidet bei der Umwandlung vom Partizipsatz der Sinn, welche Lösung gut ist (Relativsatz; Nebensatz des Grundes; Nebensatz der Zeit).**
   Überlegt z. B., ob »weil« oder »als« oder »nachdem« den Sinn am besten wiedergibt.

Schwierige Vokabeln:

aid	Hilfe	purpose	Zweck, Absicht
to apply	anwenden	to resist	widerstehen
to attempt	versuchen	scene	Schauplatz, Ort der Handlung
(the attempt)	Versuch		
to bare	entblößen, (Zähne) fletschen	sense of duty	Pflichtgefühl
		shaggy	zottig, struppig
disappointed	enttäuscht	sorrowful	sorgenvoll, traurig
growl	knurren	statement	Aussage, Erklärung
(the growl)	(Knurren)	steering-wheel	Lenkrad
to guard	bewachen	to surrender	aufgeben
to hasten	sich beeilen, eilen	possession	Besitz
incident	Zwischenfall	(to possess)	(besitzen)
to injure	sich verletzen	weapon [e]	Waffe
paw	Pfote	witness	Zeuge

Lösungen:

70.

a) leaving, rushing, baring, approaching, realizing

b) named, made, having got lost, having been injured

71.

a) A dog was arrested in the Oxford district. His name was Mick.

Lernhilfen:

69.
Grundmuster:
Nebensätze der Zeit und des Grundes, Relativsätze und verbundene Hauptsätze werden häufig durch Partizipien verkürzt.

Folgende Formen des **Partizips** sind zu beachten:
a) **Aktives Partizip**
Present participle (Mittelwort der Gegenwart): z. B. driving, leaving . . .
Perfect participle: **having** + past participle, z. B. Having done
Hier wird Vorzeitigkeit ausgedrückt: **Having arrived**, she noticed a dog.
b) **Passives Partizip**
Past participle: nam**ed**, written (3. Form des Verbs)
Perfect participle: **having been** + past participle, z. B. Having been injured. Hier ebenfalls Vorzeitigkeit!

Dog Arrested for Car Theft (1)

A dog **named** Mick was arrested in the Oxford district yesterday for stealing a car. On the basis of the statements **made** by the witnesses, the police described the incident as follows:
On a quiet country road a woman driver noticed a big, shaggy, extraordinarily sorrowful dog, **having** obviously **got lost** or **been injured**. She stopped her car and **leaving** the door open hastened to the aid of the unlucky animal. Hardly had the woman left the car when the dog got up; **rushing** past her, it jumped on to the driver's seat and put its front paws on the steering-wheel.
Again and again the lady tried to persuade the dog to get down off the seat, but without success. **Baring** its teeth it resisted all her attempts, whether gentle or ungentle, to push it away. Quite beside herself, the woman stopped a passing lorry and asked the driver for help. **Approaching** the dog, he was also greeted with growls. **Realizing** that the dog was not willing to surrender he took the disappointed Good Samaritan ten miles to the nearest police station in Oxford.

70.
Ordne die Partizipien aus dem Text in folgende Gruppen ein:

a) aktives Partizip

....

b) passives Partizip

....

71.
Find the sentence with a similar meaning and mark it with a cross:

a) A dog named Mick was arrested in the Oxford district.
☐ A dog that belonged to Mick was arrested in the Oxford district.
☐ A dog was arrested in the Oxford district. His name was Mick.
☐ Mick arrested a dog in a district named Oxford.

b) When he approached the dog, he was also greeted with growls.

72.

a) The dog rushing past the lady jumped onto the seat.

b) The policemen wanting to approach the dog were greeted with growls.

c) The inspector noted the statements made by witnesses.

d) The lorry driver wanting to help the lady stopped at once.

Kurze Wiederholung:
Relativsatz wird verkürzt!
A woman **who drove** into town noticed a dog. →
A woman **driving** into town ...
The dog **that was taken** to the police was Mick. →
The dog **taken** to the police ...
Passives Partizip!

73.

a) Before rushing into the car, the dog had been sitting on the road.

b) After having tried to convince the dog, the driver took the lady to the police station.

c) Seeing the dog, the lady stopped her car.

d) Sitting in her car, the lady noticed a dog.

Muster:
Nebensatz der Zeit wird verkürzt!
When the woman **drove** into town, she noticed a dog. →
Driving into town the woman ...
(›the dog‹ erscheint jetzt im Hauptsatz, damit wir wissen, wer gemeint ist!)

b) Approaching the dog, he was also greeted with growls.
☐ The dog approached him and greeted him with growls.
☐ When the dog approached, he was also greeted with growls.
☐ When he approached the dog, he was also greeted with growls.

72.

Shorten the relative clauses by a participial construction:

a) The dog, which rushed past the lady, jumped onto the seat.

....

b) The policemen, who wanted to approach the dog, were greeted with growls.

....

c) The inspector noted the statements which were made by witnesses.

....

d) The lorry driver, who wanted to help the lady, stopped at once.

....

73.

Shorten the adverbial clauses of time by a participial construction:

a) Before the dog rushed into the car, it had been sitting on the road.

....

b) After the driver had tried to convince the dog, he took the lady to the police station.

....

c) When the lady saw the dog, she stopped her car.

....

d) While the lady was sitting in her car, she noticed a dog.

74.

Muster:
Nebensatz des Grundes wird verkürzt!
As the woman **was** beside herself, she asked for help. →
Being beside herself, the woman . . .

as, because fallen weg!

a) Knowing that . . .

b) Fearing that . . .

75.

Zwei Hauptsätze werden verbunden! Der Sinnzusammenhang ist entscheidend für die Satzkonstruktion.

a) The lady noticed a dog rushing past her.

b) Having noticed a dog, the lady was rushing towards it.

c) The lady noticing a sorrowful dog stopped her car.

auch: Noticing a sorrowful dog the lady stopped her car.

d) A dog having stolen a car, was arrested in Oxford Street.

auch: Having stolen a car, . . .

e) Having been asked for help, the driver tried to persuade the dog.

f) Approaching the dog, the driver was greeted with growls.

74.
Shorten the adverbial clauses of reason by a participial construction:

a) As he knew that he wouldn't be able to do anything, the lorry driver rushed to the next police station.

....

....

b) As it feared that they would push it away, the dog bared its teeth.

....

....

75.
Link the two sentences by using a participial construction:

a) The lady noticed a dog. The dog was rushing past her.

....

b) The lady had noticed a dog. The lady was rushing towards the dog.

....

c) The lady stopped her car. She noticed a sorrowful dog.

....

d) A dog was arrested in Oxford Street. It had stolen a car.

....

e) The driver had been asked for help. He tried to persuade the dog.

....

f) The driver approached the dog and was greeted with growls.

....

***76.**

Muster:
Zwei verschiedene Subjekte (the dog, nobody)!

a) The dog not wanting to give in, the lady could not take her car.

b) The lady leaving her car, the dog rushed past her.

c) The animal being furious, nobody could approach the car.

77.

Hier müssen wir überlegen, welche Art von Nebensatz dem Sinn nach in Frage kommt!

a) The police who had questioned all witnesses, noted down the facts.
Relativsatz (relative clause)!

b) When the lady was driving on a quiet country road, she noticed a dog.
Nebensatz der Zeit (time clause)!

c) As she was quite beside herself, the lady stopped a lorry.
Nebensatz des Grundes (reason)! Am Beginn des Satzes steht ›as‹!

d) A big dog which was looking sorrowful, sat near a country road.
Relativsatz!

e) The dog put its paws on the steering-wheel because it wanted to guard the car.
Nebensatz des Grundes!

f) The woman was quite beside herself and asked a driver for help.
Zwei verbundene Hauptsätze!

*76.

Shorten the adverbial clauses (two different subjects!):

a) As the dog didn't want to give in, the lady couldn't take the car.

....

b) When the lady left her car, the dog rushed past her.

....

c) As the animal was furious, nobody could approach the car.

....

77.

Replace the participial construction by clauses. Choose between: as, because, who, that which, when, and

a) The police having questioned all witnesses, noted down the facts.

....

b) Driving on a quiet country road, the lady noticed a dog.

....

c) Being quite beside herself, the lady stopped a lorry.

....

d) A big dog looking sorrowful, sat near a country road.

....

e) The dog put its paws on the steering-wheel wanting to guard the car.

....

f) The woman was quite beside herself when asking a driver for help.

....

....

Comprehension Test: Dog arrested for Car Theft (2)

It was anything but easy to convince the police that a dog had taken possession of the woman's car. Finally, however, two policemen sent to the scene tried to solve the problem. They used every trick they could think of, even offering the dog a juicy sausage – a rarely-used police »weapon« indeed. Yet all they did was in vain. In the end they had to apply a certain kind of spray normally used for other purposes to overcome the »criminal«.
After having passed the night locked up in a cell, the dog was fetched next day by his mistress, a travelling saleswoman, whose car it was used to guarding. Having imagined that every car was meant to be guarded as soon as the driver had left it, the dog did not give in. Therefore, as the police inspector put it in his statement to the press, it was not a case of criminality but of an overkeen sense of duty.

78.

Mark the sentence which corresponds to the first sentence:

a) Two policemen sent to the scene tried to solve the problem.

☐ Two policemen were sent to the scene and tried to solve the problem.
☐ Two policemen who were sent to the scene tried to solve the problem.
☐ After two policemen were sent to the scene, they tried to solve the problem.

b) After having passed the night locked up in a cell, the dog was fetched by its mistress.

☐ After the night had passed, the dog was locked up in a cell and was fetched by its mistress.
☐ The night passed after the dog was locked up in a cell and was fetched by its mistress.
☐ After the dog had passed the night locked up in a cell, it was fetched by its mistress.

79.

One of the following sentences has got the same structure as:

a) They had to apply a certain spray normally **used** for other purposes.

☐ The dog was offered a juicy sausage.
☐ As the policemen had no chance left they used every trick.
☐ The police, convinced that a dog had stolen the car, went to the scene.
☐ The lady whose car it was used to guarding, fetched it next day.

b) The dog **sitting** on the driver's seat did not give in.

☐ The police was standing near and watched the dog.
☐ All the tricks being used by the police failed.
☐ Having seen the dog, the police tried to arrest it.
☐ The inspector wrote a statement being convinced that it was not a case of criminality.

80.

Shorten the subordinate clauses by using a participial construction:

a) Before the police arrived at the car, they had already made a plan.

....

b) The lady, who was on her way to town, fetched her dog.

....

c) The dog didn't give in because it thought it had to guard the car.

....

d) When the police arrived at the car, they were greeted with a growl.

....

e) As the police could not think of any other tricks, they used a spray.

....

81.

Join the following sentences by using a participal construction:

a) The police saw the lady. The police were watching the dog.

....

b) The police saw the lady. The lady was watching the dog.

....

c) The policemen were very clever. They used a special trick.

....

d) The lady went shopping. She could not take care of the dog.

....

*e) The dog did not want to give in. The police had to think of a trick.

....

82.

Replace the participial constructions by clauses:

a) Having arrived at the car the police tried to convince the dog.

....

b) The dog showing a sense of duty was no criminal.

....

c) The inspector wrote a statement being convinced that it was not a case of criminality.

....

*d) The lady having been told that the dog had been taken to the police station, was glad being allowed to fetch it.

....

I) Indirekte Rede (Indirect Speech; Reported Speech)

Fehlerquellen:

1. **Denkt an die Zeitenverschiebung, wenn das einleitende Verb in der Past Tense steht.**
   Wiederholt hierfür Übung 86)
2. **Beachtet weitere Veränderungen.**
   z. B. here → there; 87)
3. **Verwendet bei indirekten Entscheidungsfragen »if« oder »whether«.**
   z. B. John asked: »Do you often watch TV?«
   John wanted to know if (oder: whether) I often watched TV.
   Beachtet die Schreibung von whether (weather = Wetter!) und die Bedeutung von »if« in diesen Sätzen (»ob«). 88)
4. **Denkt daran, daß bei unverrückbaren Tatsachen die Zeiten nicht verschoben werden.** 90a)b)c)

Schwierige Vokabeln:

advertisement	Anzeige; Annonce
to cause	verursachen
desirable	wünschenswert
(desire)	(Wunsch)
exceptional	außergewöhnlich
(exception)	(Ausnahme)
to exclaim	ausrufen
(exclamation mark)	(Ausrufezeichen)
estate office	Immobilienbüro
to glance at	e. Blick werfen auf
to outgrow	herauswachsen
(to grow)	(wachsen)
picturesque	malerisch
(picture)	(Bild)
pleasant [e]	angenehm, erfreulich
spacious	geräumig
(space)	(Raum)
to suggest	vorschlagen
uproar	Aufruhr

Lösungen: | **Lernhilfen:**

83.

Grundmuster:

Bei der Umwandlung von der **direkten** (direct speech) in die **indirekte Rede** (indirect speech oder reported speech) beachten wir zunächst, daß sich die **Pronomen** je nach Sinnzusammenhang ändern:

Tom says, »**I am** ill.« →
Tom says (that) **he is** ill.

Beachte auch die Satzzeichen!

Reporting verbs (einleitende Verben) sind:
to add, to agree, to announce, to answer, to ask, to declare, to exclaim, to observe, to promise, to remark, to reply, to say, to shout, to wonder, . . .

84.

announced, exclaimed, said, remarked

85.

Steht das ›**reporting verb**‹ im **Present, Present Perfect** oder **Future,** wird die Zeit **nicht** verändert.
›Reporting verb‹ im Present!

a) Mrs. Nolan says that she wants a bigger house.

b) Sam adds that he needs a room of his own.

A Home to their Liking

One morning at breakfast Mrs. Nolan caused an uproar when she announced, »Let's find a bigger house somewhere else in the city, I think we've outgrown this one.« »But, Mother, we like it here!« exclaimed the three young Nolans. »Oh, we'll find a larger place you'll like just as well,« said Mrs. Nolan. »Judy is old enough to have her own room and your grandmother is also coming to live with us.« »I guess we'll have to look for a larger place,« remarked Mr. Nolan. »I'll stop in at Mr. Bardon's estate office and speak to him about buying a new house and selling our old one.«

Each evening Mrs. Nolan would make a list of desirable houses for sale as soon as the newspaper came, but some were too small, others needed cleaning and redecorating or they were too expensive.

On Sunday morning Mrs. Nolan ran down to get the Sunday paper. After glancing at the ›Homes for Sale‹ page she hurried upstairs. »Sam, Mr. Bardon has just the right house,« she said. »Listen to this: Lovely picturesque home, exceptionally pleasant, three bedrooms, spacious living-room, modern kitchen with breakfast-room, modern bath upstairs, comfortable stairway leading to a light, roomy attic large enough for a further room.«

84.
Find the reporting verbs from the text:

....

85.
Put into reported speech:

a) Mrs. Nolan <u>says</u>, »I want a bigger house.«

....

b) Sam <u>adds</u>, »I need a room of my own.«

....

c) Judy has said (that) they'll have to find a house with six rooms.

›Reporting verb‹ im Present Perfect ...

d) Mr. Nolan will declare that he will buy a new house.

... bzw. im Future!

86.

Erweiterung des Grundmusters:
Steht das **einleitende Verb** (reporting verb) im **Past Tense** oder **Past Perfect,** dann ändern sich die Zeiten bei der Umwandlung von der **direkten** in die **indirekte Rede:**

Present Tense	→	**Past Tense**
Present Perfect	→	**Past Perfect**
Past Tense	→	**Past Perfect**
Future	→	**Conditional**
Future Perfect	→	**Conditional Perfect**

a) Mrs. Nolan said (that) she wanted a bigger house.

b) Sam added (that) he had seen an advertisement in the paper.

c) Judy had said (that) she had always wanted a room of her own.

d) Mrs. Nolan said (that) they would buy a house if they had the money.

e) Mr. Nolan declared (that) he would buy a new house and sell the old one.

f) Mr. Nolan said (that) he would stop in at the estate office to see Mr. Bardon and would speak to him about buying a new house.

Beachte: Mr. Nolan said ... steht am Anfang. Die beiden Sätze der direkten Rede werden in der indirekten Rede mit ›**and**‹ verbunden.

c) Judy has said, »We'll have to find a house with six rooms.«

....

d) Mr. Nolan will declare, »I'll buy a new house.«

....

86.

Change into reported speech:

a) Mrs. Nolan said: »I want a bigger house.«

....

b) Sam added: »I saw an advertisement in the paper.«

....

c) Judy had said: »I've always wanted a room of my own.«

....

d) Mrs. Nolan said: »We will buy a house if we have the money.«

....

e) Mr. Nolan declared: »I'll buy a new house and sell the old one.«

....

....

f) »I'll stop in at the estate office to see Mr. Bardon,« said Mr. Nolan.
»I'll speak to him about buying a new house.«

....

....

....

*87.

a) Mr. Nolan said (that) he didn't like that place any more.

b) She added (that) they had been reading all those advertisements.

c) Her husband mentioned (that) he didn't like it there either.

d) Then he added (that) he woul have a look at the newspaper that day.

e) Sam said (that) his friend had shown him his room the day before.

f) Judy remarked (that) she had been shown his room two days before.

g) Grandmother declared (that) she would move out the next day.

h) Father replied (that) they would have a larger house the following week.

i) Grandmother said (that) he had just said the same the previous month.

j) Mrs. Nolan said (that) they had missed a good chance a year before.

Beachte: Weitere Veränderungen bei der Umwandlung von **direkter** zu **indirekter Rede**:

this → that

these → those

here → there

today → that day

yesterday → the day before

the day before yesterday → two days before

tomorrow → the next day/the following day

next week/year . . . → the following week/year . . .

last month → the previous month

a year ago → a year before/the previous year

*87.

Put into reported speech (Mind the words in bold print!):

a) Mr. Nolan said: »I don't like **this** place any more.«

....

b) She added: »We were reading all **these** advertisements.«

....

c) Her husband mentioned: »I don't like it **here** either.«

....

d) Then he added: »I'll have a look at the newspaper **today.**«

....

e) Sam said: »My friend showed me his room **yesterday.**«

....

f) Judy remarked: »And I was shown his room **the day before yesterday.**«

....

g) Grandmother declared: »I'll move out **tomorrow.**«

....

h) Father replied: »We'll have a larger house **next** week.«

....

i) »**Last** month you just said the same,« said grandmother.

....

j) Mrs. Nolan said: »We missed a good chance a year **ago.**«

....

88.

a) Sam asked why they moved.

b) Judy wondered where the house was situated.

c) Mr. Nolan asked why he should go to an estate agent.

d) Mrs. Nolan inquired how many rooms they would need.

e) Mr. Nolan asked what sort of house she (they) would buy.

f) Sam asked his father if he had an offer.

g) Mrs. Nolan wondered whether they (he, she) had already seen the house.

h) Judy asked her father if the estate agent had shown him a plan of the house.

i) Mother asked her children if they had been happy when they had heard about their new idea.

j) Judy wondered whether they would have enough rooms in their new house.

Beachte: **Wortstellung** im indirekten Fragesatz: **S – P – O**!
Kein Fragezeichen!

Beachte: **say** wird in der indirekten Frage zu **ask, wonder, inquire, want to know, . . .**
Bei **Entscheidungsfragen** (Antwort ist »ja« oder »nein«) wird der indirekte Fragesatz mit **whether** oder **if** eingeleitet, da ja kein Fragepronomen vorhanden ist.

88.

Put the following questions into reported speech:

a) Sam asked: »Why do we move?«

....

b) Judy wondered: »Where is the house situated?«

....

c) Mr. Nolan asked: »Why shall I go to an estate office?«

....

d) Mrs. Nolan inquired: »How many rooms will we need?«

....

e) Mr. Nolan said: »What sort of house will you buy?«

....

f) Sam asked his father: »Do you have an offer?"

....

g) Mrs. Nolan wondered: »Have you already seen the house?«

....

h) Judy asked her father: »Did the estate agent show you a plan of the house?«

....

i) Mother asked her children: »Were you happy when you heard about our new idea?«

....

....

j) Judy wondered: »Will we have enough rooms in our new house?«

....

89.

a) Mrs. Nolan told Sam to listen to her.

Enthält die direkte Rede einen Befehl oder eine Aufforderung, so wird das einleitende Verb ›say‹ in der indirekten Rede zu: **tell, order, command, ask, . . .**

b) Judy told Sam to leave her alone.

Beachte: Angesprochene Person muß genannt werden!

c) Sam shouted (that) she should not always lose her temper.

Sinn entscheidet, wer gemeint ist! (hier: Judy → she)

d) Father told them to stop quarrelling.

gemeint sind Judy und Sam → them!

e) Mrs. Nolan told Sam that when he had finished, he was to go upstairs.

auch: Mrs. N. told Sam to go upstairs when he had finished.

*90.

a) Judy said (that) there are four countries in the United Kingdom – . . .

b) Sam stated that London lies on the Thames.

c) The boy remarked that one year is 365 days.

(a–c) Unverrückbare Tatsachen: **keine Änderung** der Zeiten!

d) Mrs. Nolan suggested that they should have a look at the newspaper.

Vorschlag (suggestion)!

89.
Put the following imperatives into reported speech:

a) Mrs. Nolan <u>said to</u> Sam: »Listen to me.«

....

b) Judy said: »Leave me alone, <u>Sam</u>.«

....

c) Sam shouted: »Don't always lose your temper.«

....

d) Father said: »Stop quarrelling.«

....

*e) Mrs. Nolan said to Sam: »When you've finished, go upstairs.«

....

....

*90.
Some special cases:

a) Judy said: »There are four countries in the United Kingdom – England, Scotland, Wales and Northern Ireland.«

....

b) Sam stated: »London lies on the Thames.«

....

c) The boy remarked: »One year is 365 days.«

....

d) Mrs. Nolan said: »Let's have a look at the newspaper.«

....

e) The children suggested that they should stop quarrelling then.	to suggest = vorschlagen now → then
f) Sam thanked his father.	to thank = danken
g) Judy wished the family a good morning.	Wunsch (wish)!
h) Mrs. Nolan asked Sam if he could make a list of houses and he said he couldn't.	Frage (to ask)! Hilfsverb muß wiederholt werden! (could)
i) Mrs. Nolan asked Mr. Nolan whether he would have time to read the advertisements and he said he would.	Hilfsverb wiederholen! (would)
j) He asked which one I would choose and I said I would choose the large one.	Verbform ›I would choose‹ wiederholen!
k) He called the boys.	
l) She told him to charge a good price if he bought the house.	Befehl zuerst!

e) The children said: »Let's stop quarrelling now.«

....

f) Sam said: »Thank you.« (After his father had given him the newspaper)

....

g) Judy said: »Good morning.« (The family was already sitting at the breakfast table)

....

h) Mrs. Nolan said: »Can you make a list of houses?« and Sam said, »No.«

....

....

i) Mrs. Nolan said: »Will you have time to read the advertisements?« and Mr. Nolan said, »Yes.«

....

....

j) »Which one will you choose?« he asked. »The large one,« I said.

....

....

k) He said, »Come here, boys.«

....

l) She said, »If you buy the house, charge a good price.«

....

....

91.

Bei dieser Art von Übungen handelt es sich um eine Umwandlung von **indirekter** in **direkte Rede**. Hier fallen die einleitenden Verben (asked, told, ...) weg!

Have you got any houses for sale?

I've got quite a number of houses which I think could suit you.

›could‹ wird nicht umgewandelt!

How much will we have to pay and what price can we get for our old one?

That depends on the size you need, the number of rooms you want and where the house is situated.

I will let you know after we have discussed this problem in our family.

91.

Write down the dialogue between Mr. Nolan and Mr. Bardon:

Mr. Nolan comes back home and tells his family about his visit at the estate agent's, Mr. Bardon:
»First I asked him if he had got any houses for sale.

Mr. Nolan: » .... ?«

Mr. Bardon told me that he had got quite a number of houses which he thought could suit us.

Mr. Bardon: » ....

....«

Then I wanted to know how much we would have to pay for a new house and what price we could get for our old one.

Mr. Nolan: » ....

.... ?«

Mr. Bardon explained to me that it depended on the size we needed, the number of rooms we wanted and where the house was situated.

Mr. Bardon: » ....

....«

In the end I told him that I would let him know after we had discussed that problem in our family.«

Mr. Nolan: » ....

....«

Comprehension Test: A Home to their Liking (part two)

When Mrs. Nolan had read out the advertisement from the newspaper, she asked: »What do you think about that?« »That does sound attractive,« agreed Mr. Nolan. »However, it doesn't say where and how much it is. I'll call Mr. Bardon about it.« Mr. Nolan telephoned and all the Nolans stood near, listening. »Mr. Bardon, this is Mr. Nolan. My wife has just read your advertisement in today's paper. There's one house she thinks will suit us. It's the fifth in your list. ——— What are you laughing about sir?« asked Mr. Nolan. Then he laughed too, and hung up. »What did he say?« asked Mrs. Nolan eagerly. »Where's the house? « »I've got a surprise for you, Mother«, said Mr. Nolan. »The house in the advertisement is our own.« »Oh,« exclaimed Steve. »I didn't know we had all these things. Read it again Mother, please.« Mrs. Nolan read the advertisement aloud again. Then she said, »Do you know, this advertisement does give me an idea. We can convert the southwest corner of the attic into a big room for the boys.« »Hurrah!« shouted the three small Nolans. »We won't have to move.«

92.

Answer the following questions (Answer in reported speech!):

a) What did Mrs. Nolan ask when she had read out the advertisement?

She asked ....

b) What did Mr. Nolan ask Mr. Bardon?

....

*c) What did Steve exclaim?

....

*d) What did the three small Nolans shout?

....

93.

Choose the right sentence:

a) Mrs. Nolan asked eagerly: »What did he say?«
This sentence in indirect speech is: Mrs. Nolan asked eagerly

☐ what he would say. ☐ what he will say.
☐ what he had said. ☐ what he said.

b) Mrs. Nolan said: »We can convert the attic.«
This sentence in indirect speech is: Mrs. Nolan said

☐ that they can convert the attic. ☒ that they could convert the attic.
☐ that we could convert the attic. ☐ that they would convert the attic.

94.

Rewrite the following in reported speech:

a) »That does sound attractive,« agreed Mr. Nolan.

....

b) Mr. Nolan asked: »Where's the house we want to buy?«

....

c) Sam exclaims: »None of us wants to move!«

....

d) Mrs. Nolan said to her husband: »Do you know, the advertisement does give me an idea.«

....

....

*e) Steve wanted to know: »Dad, have you seen that house and is it really as lovely as Mum told us?«

....

....

95.

Put the following dialogue between Sam and Judy into reported speech:
(Find suitable reporting verbs in the Past Tense)

Judy: »Do you know that Mum is looking for a new house?«

Judy asked Sam ....

Sam: »I heard her talking about this matter yesterday.«

....

Judy: »Isn't it terrible?«

....

Sam: »Yes, it's no good idea to move out.«

....

Judy: »Do you know how much a new house will cost?«

....

Sam: »No, I don't; but I think that we can't afford buying a new one.«

....

Judy: »If we voted against this plan, Mum and Dad couldn't refuse our proposals.«

....

....

Sam: »What are you going to propose?«

....

Judy: »We could convert the attic into a big room.«

....

Sam: »Oh! That's wonderful. I will immediately tell Steve.«

....

K) Adjektiv – Adverb (Adjective – Adverb)

Fehlerquellen:

1. **Haltet »as« und »than« auseinander.**
   Also: Tom is **as** tall **as** his brother. . . . **so** groß **wie** . . .
   Jane is taller **than** her sister. . . . **größer als** . . .
2. **Schreibt »than« richtig.**
   Also: taller than; aber: Then = dann, damals
3. **Merkt euch die unregelmäßigen Steigerungsformen.**
   Also: bad – worse – worst
   good – better – best
   far – farther/further – farthest/furthest und andere!
4. **Beachtet die unterschiedlichen Formen von Adjektiv und Adverb, die es im Deutschen so nicht gibt.**
   Also: Tom is clever. He is a clever boy. He acts cleverly.
   = Tom ist klug. Er ist ein kluger Bub. Er handelt klug.
5. **Merkt euch, daß sich das Adverb der Art und Weise (= Adverb of Manner) auf ein Verb** – Tom acts cleverly (Wie arbeitet er?)
   . . . ein Adjektiv – Tom is really clever. (Wie klug ist er?)
   . . . ein anderes Adverb – He writes really quickly. (Wie schnell schreibt er?)
   . . . oder einen ganzen Satz – Fortunately, we were not alone.
   beziehen kann.
6. **Achtet auf die Rechtschreibung.**
   z. B. complete → completely; definite → definitely
   Das e fällt weg bei true → truly; whole → wholly; simple → simply und anderen Adjektiven, die auf -le enden.

Schwierige Vokabeln:

administration	Regierung	independence	Unabhängigkeit
average	Durchschnitt, durchschnittlich	means	Mittel
		minority	Minderheit
belief	Glaube	poverty	Armut
(to believe)	(glauben)	privileged	bevorrechtet
custom	Brauch	reason	Grund, Ursache
desperate	verzweifelt	to retain	beibehalten
to expect	erwarten	stress	Betonung
health	Gesundheit	to threaten [e]	drohen
housing	Unterkunft, Wohnung	violent	gewaltsam

Lösungen:	Lernhilfen:
	96. **Kurze Wiederholung:** a) America is a **large** country. (**Adjektiv** als Attribut zu einem Substantiv!) Many Indians are **poor**. (**Adjektiv als Prädikatsnomen!**) b) He does his job **well.** (**Adverb** zur näheren Bestimmung eines Verbs!)
97. nearly, economically, socially, educationally, likely	Grundmuster: Adjektiv + -ly → Adverb (social + -ly → socially) Es gibt auch Adverbien, die nicht auf -ly enden; z. B.: quite, always, yesterday, only.
98. a) many; more b) better; best c) bad; worse d) likely; most likely	

A People with a Right to Protest

Most American Indians have **good** reason to protest: in that **great rich** continent, they are the minority group in the **worst** position. There are **nearly** a million Indians, who are the only **native** Americans. **Most** of them live in mid-west and west coast states. **Economically**, **socially** and **educationally**, they are **less privileged** than anybody else in the United States. Indians can expect to live till they are 44; everybody else in the U.S.A. can expect to live till they are 64. Their **average** income is below ›poverty level‹. An Indian baby is three times **more likely** to die than any other. Indians have the **highest** alcoholic rate, the **lowest** standard of education, the **poorest** health conditions and the **worst** housing.

97.

The words in bold print are either adjectives or adverbs. Write down the adverbs.

....

....

98.

Find the missing forms:

Positive	Comparative	Superlative
a)	....	**most** (Indians)
b) **good** (reason)	....	....
c)	....	(the) **worst** (position)
d)	**more likely** (to die)	....

e) high; higher

f) poor; poorer

g) little; least

99.

Vergleich im Satz:
Tom is **as tall as** Jack.
Tom is **not so tall as** Jim.
Mary is **taller than** Susan.
Mary is **more intelligent than** Jenny.

Jenny is **less intelligent than** Susan.
Tom is **the tallest** boy in his class.
Tom is **the most intelligent** boy in his class.

Steigerung der Adverbien:
slowly – more slowly – most slowly
badly – worse – worst
→ **Schulbuch**

a) larger than

b) as big as (so big as)

c) more; than

d) fewer; than

e) more likely; than

f) less privileged than

g) higher; than

h) worse than

i) more important than

e) .... (the) **highest** (rate)

f) .... (the) **poorest** (conditions)

g) .... **less** (privileged) ....

99.

Fill in the correct form of the adjective or adverb and »as«, »so«, »than«, as required.

a) America is .... Europe. (**large**)

b) Europe is not .... America. (**big**)

c) There are .... white Americans .... American Indians. (**many**)

d) .... Indians live in east coast states .... in mid-west or west coast states. (**few**)

e) White Americans are .... to live longer .... Indians. (**likely**)

f) Indians are .... white people. (**privileged**)

g) White Americans have a .... standard of education

.... Indians. (**high**)

h) Indians are treated .... anybody else. (**badly**)

i) Building hospitals and schools for Indians is ....

.... building hotels for tourists. (**important**)

100.

	Beachte die unregelmäßigen Steigerungsformen dieser Adjektive bzw. Zahlwörter!
a) Most; much	
much	
b) few	Nach **much** bzw. **little folgt** das Substantiv **im Singular**, nach **many** bzw. **few** aber **im Plural**!
Little	
c) farther; than	
further	

101.

a) desperately	Adverb ›desperately‹ bestimmt ›bad‹ genauer!
b) in a friendly way	**Adjektive auf -ly** bilden das Adverb durch Umschreibung!
c) hard	hard = schwer, hart; hardly = kaum
d) hard	
e) terribly high	it **is** (to be!) high
f) remarkably poor	
g) badly	
h) extremely low	= äußerst niedrig
i) highly interesting	= höchst interessant

100.
Fill in the correct forms of »much/many«, »little/few«, »far«:

a) .... Indians don't earn as .... as white people. An Indian child hasn't .... of a chance to get a good education.

b) Only .... Indians get a chance to study at a college. .... has been done to help the Indians.

c) America is .... away from Germany .... Austria. Who wants to make .... remarks on this topic?

101.
Adjective or adverb?

a) I read about the .... bad conditions of the native Americans. (**desperate**)
b) Most Indians have not always been treated .... (**friendly**)
c) Life in the reservations is very .... (**hard**)
d) The government did not try very .... to improve the situation. (**hard**)
e) The alcoholic rate of Indians is .... (**terrible, high**)
f) The health conditions are .... (**remarkable, poor**)
g) A great many Indians are educated .... (**bad**)
h) The standard of education is .... (**extreme, low**)
i) The article was .... (**high, interesting**).

102.

Nach einigen Verben (z. B.: **to become, to get, to grow, to look, to seem, to remain**) folgt das **Adjektiv**! (vergleiche **to be**!)

a) unsatisfactory

b) hungry — look = aussehen (= sein!)

c) sadly

d) angrily — look at = anschauen (Wie?)

e) probable — Adjektiv auch nach: to sound, to smell, to taste!

f) justly

103.

a) Je mehr ich . . ., desto mehr . . .

b) Es ist sehr schwierig . . . — auch: außergewöhnlich, äußerst

c) Das schwierigste Problem . . .

d) Krankenhäuser und Schulen zu bauen, ist etwas Gutes.

e) Die Lage wird immer schwieriger. — ähnlich: better and better = immer besser

102.
Which form is correct?

a) The situation of many Indians seems rather .... **(unsatisfactory, unsatisfactorily)**

b) The Indian baby looked .... **(hungry, hungrily)**

c) After I had seen an Indian village I went home .... **(sad, sadly)**

d) The Indian girl looked .... at the strangers. **(angry, angrily)**

e) Your report of America sounds .... **(probable, probably)**
wahrscheinlich

f) It shows that the Indians have not been treated .... **(just, justly)**.
gerecht

103.
Translate into German:

a) **The** more I learn about the U.S.A., **the** more I want to know.

....

b) It is **most difficult** to get books on Indian culture in my home town.

....

....

c) **The most difficult** problem for many Indians are health conditions.

....

d) Building hospitals and schools is **a good thing.**

....

e) The situation is getting **more and more difficult.**

....

Comprehension Test: A People with a Right to Protest (part two)

When the white settlers came, the Indians lost much of their rich land and many of their customs and beliefs. During the Eisenhower administration (1953–1961), the central government tried to force the Indians to integrate; less money was given to the reservations and the hungry Indians came to the cities – just as the government wanted.
Now the Indians are desperately trying to preserve their cultural character and independence. At most colleges in the West there are studies on the Indian tribes; regional Indian organisations want American history to be taught with more stress on the Indian culture. Things are moving, but not fast enough for the radicals. In the year 1974 the Indians threatened the sheriff and all the other representatives of white bureaucratic power with their guns at Wounded Knee, South Dakota. They want things now, not later. And if they don't get them now by peaceful means, they feel they have the right to take them by force.

104.

Give the comparatives and superlatives: (adjectives and adverbs!)

a) **rich** ....

b) **hungry** ....

c) **desperately** ....

d) **fast** ....

e) **peaceful** ....

105.

True or false according to the text?

	T	F
a) The government hadn't expected the hungry Indians to come to the big cities.	☐	☐
b) The Indians don't want to stick to their culture.	☐	☐
c) Students can get information on the history of the Indians at a great many colleges.	☐	☐
d) Some radical Indians want things to improve more rapidly.	☐	☐
e) A most serious incident happened at Wounded Knee, South Dakota.	☐	☐

106.

Complete so that the following statements make sense:

a) Today the Indians have .... rich land .... before the white settlers came. **(little)**

b) Before 1953 the situation for the Indians was ....

.... in the years to come. **(serious)**

c) Today colleges are .... in Indian culture .... they were before. **(interested)**

d) Things are not moving .... some radicals hope. **(fast)**

e) The .... incident was at Wounded Knee. **(serious)**

107.
Adjective or adverb?

a) The government tried **(hard, hardly)** .... to force the Indians to integrate.

b) Many Indians .... arrived in the cities **(hungry, hungrily)**.

c) The situation for them was rather **(desperate, desperately)** ....
....

d) They were not always treated **(fair, fairly)** ....

e) Today they are **(intensive, intensively)** .... trying to keep their independence.

f) Many Indians want to get their rights **(peaceful, peacefully)** ....
....

g) Some radicals feel **(unhappy, unhappily)** ....; they want to take their rights **(violent, violently)** ....

108.
Translate:

a) The situation of many Indians is most serious.

....

b) The Sioux are one of the most famous Indian tribes.

....

c) The sooner the American government changes things the better.

....

....

Alphabetisches Verzeichnis der wichtigsten grammatischen Ausdrücke aus den Übungen

Wir üben
Hilfsverben

19.

has to; has; being; would be; can; has; can; am; may

20.

a) cannot (can't)
b) must not
c) must
d) shall we (build)
e) can you (understand)
f) need not

21.

a) will have to save
b) could not understand
c) had to be done
d) this work might lead to a terrible end.

22.

a) People didn't work less in the past.
b) We ought not to forget the dangers of atomic energy.
c) I don't know all about atomic power stations.
d) We must not stay in this part of the factory.
e) We can't learn all about physics in four years at school.

23.

a) Wir sollten über Cyril Garbetts Worte nachdenken.
b) Was sollen wir nun machen?
c) Was mußt du hier machen?
d) Ich bin sicher, wir könnten eine Menge Geld sparen.
e) Sie hätten eine Menge Geld sparen können, wenn sie vorsichtiger gewesen wären.

Wir üben
Aktiv und Passiv

29.
a) A new source of energy has been found by scientists.
b) Large quantities of energy are released by splitting uranium atoms.
c) The natural resources will be used up in a few years' time.

30.
a) will be used up
b) is needed
c) are being made

31.
a) Oil is said to be better for heating than coal. (It is said that...)
b) Large quantities of energy are released by uranium atoms.
c) A new way of getting atomic energy will have been found in ten years' time.
d) In the near future plenty of cheap energy will be produced.
e) Energy ought to be saved by everybody.
f) Scientists are said to be solving the problems of energy.
g) Has that problem ever been thought about?
h) That problem would not have been thought about if energy had not run short recently.
i) If the heating in our country was turned down a little, 10 per cent of the oil could be saved.

32.
a) Scientists (They) have taken another step towards the development of new sources of energy.
b) Scientists can develop new ways of using atomic energy.
c) The leading nations must save most of the energy which they use before they use up all the natural resources.
d) Have they (people) already tested these possibilities?

Wir üben Konditionalsätze

37.

a) If I wanted to get away from the big seaside resorts I could choose one of the small islands around Britain.
b) If I really travel to Britain, I will see London and Edinburgh.
c) If I come in August, the Edinburgh Festival will be held.

38.

a) would stay
b) had known
c) must go
d) won't be able to say

39.

a) ask
b) were
c) saved
d) says

40.

a) I would like to spend my holidays in Britain.
b) will be able to see
c) want to fly
d) had not been told

41.

will be coming; will ... give; pass; learnt; were; would pay attention; would be glad; would not remind.

Wir üben
Infinitivkonstruktionen

49.

a) The teacher tells him to do his homework carefully.
b) It is not easy for him to learn Hebrew.
c) The teacher tells them what to do.

50.

a) His parents want him to go on to university.
b) Most parents expect their children to work hard at school.
c) The teachers advise us to do exercises.
d) Mr. Brown permits the boy to leave earlier.
e) My friend has persuaded me to take Greek as an optional subject.
f) I can hardly believe her to be the best student.

... Bill to try ...

51.

a) This is the best method which can be thought of.
b) This is the most useful book on grammar which can be bought.
c) Tom and Susan were the last students who left the room. hall
d) For Tom English is the most interesting subject which can be chosen.
e) This was the worst play which was performed at our school.

52.

a) Children usually don't understand how to work efficiently.
b) You must always tell them what to do and how to do it.
c) The teacher told Bob when to do his homework.
d) The newcomers wanted to know where to go to school.

53.

a) The text is too difficult for the students to read.
b) It is necessary for us to learn different structures.
c) It was very kind of him to help the old lady.
d) The suitcase was too heavy for the old lady to carry.

Wir üben
Gerund

64.
He was looking forward to seeing his family.
It is worth while visiting London.
He enjoyed travelling home.

65.
a) Ich hatte meinen letzten Tag in London mit Einkaufen verbracht.
b) Ich freute mich darauf, meine Familie wieder zu sehen.
c) Die Tatsache, daß ich mich ziemlich unbehaglich fühlte, war nicht zu leugnen.
d) Die Beamten entschuldigten sich dafür, daß sie mein Gepäck untersuchten.

66.
a) He was very keen on getting back to Britain.
b) He had no chance of explaining the ticking in the case.
c) He didn't object to opening the suitcase.
d) At last the police officers succeeded in finding something.
e) The tourist couldn't help smiling.

67.
a) going
b) visiting/to visit
c) staying
d) to disappear; being; to walk
e) looking; comparing
f) thinking over / to think over

68.
a) by hurrying
b) without causing
c) in case of missing

Wir üben
Partizipialsätze

78.

a) Two policemen who were sent to the scene tried to solve the problem.

b) After the dog had passed the night locked up in a cell, it was fetched by its mistress.

79.

a) The police, convinced that a dog had stolen the car, went to the scene.

b) All the tricks being used by the police failed.

80.

a) Before arriving at the car they had already made a plan.

b) The lady being on her way to town, fetched her dog.

c) The dog didn't give in thinking it had to guard the car.

d) Arriving at the car the police were greeted with a growl.

e) Not being able to think of any other trick the police used a spray.

81.

a) The police, watching the dog, saw the lady.

b) The police saw the lady watching the dog.

c) The policemen being very clever used a special trick.

d) The lady not being able to take care of the dog, went shopping.

*e) The dog not wanting to give in, the police had to think of a trick.

82.

a) After the police had arrived at the car, they tried to convince the dog.

b) The dog which showed a sense of duty was no criminal.

c) The inspector wrote a statement because he was convinced that it was not a case of criminality.

*d) The lady who had been told that the dog had been taken to the police station, was glad when she was allowed to fetch it.

Wir üben indirekte Rede

92.

a) She asked what they thought about that.
b) Mr. Nolan asked Mr. Bardon what he was laughing about.
*c) Steve exclaimed with surprise that he hadn't known that they had had all those things. He asked his mother to read it again.
*d) The three small Nolans expressed their joy and shouted that they would not have to move.

93.

a) Mrs. Nolan asked eagerly what he had said.
b) Mrs. Nolan said that they could convert the attic.

94.

a) Mr. Nolan agreed that that did sound attractive.
b) Mr. Nolan asked where the house was they wanted to buy.
c) Sam exclaims that none of them wants to move.
d) Mrs. Nolan asked her husband if he knew that the advertisement did give her an idea.
*e) Steve wanted to know of Dad if he had seen that house and if it was really as lovely as Mum had told them.

95.

Judy asked Sam if he knew that Mum was looking for a new house.
Sam answered that he had heard her talking about that matter the day before.
Judy asked if it was not terrible.
Sam replied that it was, and that it was no good idea to move out.
Judy wanted to know if he knew how much a new house would cost.
Sam answered that he didn't and that he thought that they could not afford buying a new one.
Judy proposed that if they voted against that plan, Mum and Dad couldn't refuse their proposals.
Sam asked what she was going to propose.
Judy answered that they could convert the attic into a big room.
Sam exclaimed that that was wonderful and that he would immediately tell Steve.

Wir üben
Adjektive und Adverbien

104.
a) richer, richest
b) hungrier, hungriest
c) more desperately, most desperately
d) faster, fastest
e) more peaceful, most peaceful

105.
a) True
b) False
c) True
d) True
e) True

106.
a) less . . . than
e) less serious . . . than (not so serious . . . as)
c) more interested . . . than
d) as fast as
e) most serious

107.
a) hard
b) hungrily
c) desperate
d) fairly
e) intensively
f) peacefully
g) unhappy; violently

108.
a) Die Lage vieler Indianer ist sehr ernst.
b) Die Sioux sind einer der berühmtesten Indianerstämme.
c) Je eher die amerikanische Regierung die Dinge ändert, desto besser.